THE
BEGINNING
OF THE END

A PRACTICAL GUIDE TO RETIREMENT PREPARATION FOR THE SMALL BUSINESS OWNER

DR TERRI BOURNE

First published in Great Britain by Practical Inspiration
Publishing, 2020

© Dr Terri Bourne, 2020

The moral rights of the author have been asserted

ISBN 978-1-78860-188-7 (print)
978-1-78860-187-0 (epub)
978-1-78860-186-3 (mobi)

Every effort has been made to trace copyright holders and to obtain their permission for the use of copyright material. The publisher apologizes for any errors or omissions and would be grateful if notified of any corrections that should be incorporated in future reprints or editions of this book.

Table of contents

Preface

Have you ever thought it might be time to sell your small business or step down a little but you're not sure where to start?

Are friends and business associates starting to sell up their businesses, change the way they work or even retire?

Are you in a dilemma about whether you should sell, when you should sell, whether this is a good 'business' decision or whether it's a good idea for your family or circumstances?

If so, *The Beginning of the End* has been written for you. For those of you who have just started to think about selling your small business, it will help you to clarify and put things into perspective. You'll be able to decide if this is a good idea, and if it is, how to make your business fit for sale, achieving the best possible returns to make your next move.

The Beginning of the End is different from your usual book about retirement. It is written for the business person in the stage *before* – for someone who is contemplating their options, seeking a bit of clarification and sizing up their opportunities.

The book will not tell you whether retirement, selling up or keeping your business is your best option. That would be an impossible task without information specific to your business and personal goals. But I am convinced that by reading this book you will feel more confident in your next decision about where your business is or should be going, and whether retirement or selling your business is part of that.

The Beginning of the End will guide your thoughts so that you can make the best decision, at the right time, for you and your business. Your mind will be challenged to consider different options in the earliest stages of considering your exit plan. It's never too early to think this through.

Even at business start-up, business owners are advised to have an exit strategy, but it is rare that any of us do. Starting with the end in mind is great advice. It helps us to know where we are heading and how to get off the business 'merry-go-round'. The reality, however, is that we often get so involved in our businesses that we are not even able to look up or 'step out' once in a while, to take note of what the rest of the world is doing.

Introduction

What made you pick up this book today? Is there something that you have been gently mulling over in your mind for some time? Do you know friends and business colleagues who have retired? Are they posting happy photos on Facebook and other social media showing them loving life now that they are not working? Well, this could be you. It may seem like a long way off due to your present situation, but everyone has to start somewhere. And with this book in your hand, you are in the best place to start.

Don't think that by reading this book you will give up your business tomorrow and retire off into the sunset. You might, of course, but the likelihood is rather slim. Unfortunately, just as you have worked hard over the years to build up your business for you and your family, you have to work hard to retire from it as well.

There's no quick fix or magic wand, although I must admit I do daydream about someone coming along and making me an offer I can't refuse, so I can jet off into the sunset... But as great as that sounds, the reality is that you'll probably have to work just as hard at moving out of your business as you have done to build it up to the business it is now.

About the author

After a successful career in teaching and school management, I had a yearning ambition to set up my own business. Enjoying the challenge of starting a business from scratch, I went on to set up seven different ventures over a ten-year period, all running concurrently, one of which had 16 branches. Relying heavily on building good staff teams and devising business systems to take each company forward, this book is based on many years' experience.

More recently, I have turned my attention to look at exit planning, retirement and beyond. My current research has led me to believe that many business owners concentrate their efforts on building and running their businesses but fail to look at how to exit them. As an entrepreneur who has worked for many years building up businesses, I am now in a good position to help you relinquish yours in the best possible way.

Open your mind

Throughout the book, you will be guided through a process, helping you to think of all the possibilities around selling your business and retiring from it. You may decide at the end of the process not to sell your business – and that's OK too. This book is about getting your business in tip-top condition to sell, so that all your hard work over the years really pays off. But probably more importantly, it's about getting you into the right frame of mind to take this enormous step – making sure that it is the right decision for you, your family and your business.

You will need an open mind to consider the possibilities. At the end of the day, if selling is not for you, hopefully you will have learned a lot from reading the book and going through the process. You are completely in charge of your destiny, just like you have always been as an entrepreneur.

One of the reasons that business owners start to think about these decisions is that they see contemporaries suffering strokes, heart attacks and worse, all whilst working themselves into the ground, on their business 'merry-go-round', thinking they are unable to get off due to their business needing them (and/or maybe them needing their business?).

If you feel you need a change of direction, this is a good place to start. Be open-minded; try some of the exercises and worksheets in the free Workbook, which you can find on my website at terribourne.com. No one is judging you. No one will see what you have written or what you are thinking about. You don't have to do anything… Or you could do a lot and get your business ready to give you the final payback.

Sound familiar?

For many years as a business owner and entrepreneur, I didn't take a wage, eventually moving on to a pittance. I worked 12- to 14-hour days, for six or sometimes seven days a week, even though I had a young family to care for. I became a 'Jack of all Trades' whilst learning to keep my head above water. I felt (and still feel) an enormous amount of responsibility for my staff and colleagues. At the time, I believed that this was just business and how it was. If I worked hard enough, I could move myself out of the hand-to-mouth situation into a more comfortable business existence – and yes, that has now happened.

But now I feel that the business owes me for all those hardship years, not only for me but my family as well. So I have considered retirement, selling the business and moving on to something else (I'm too young to 'retire-retire'). But before I go, I need the business to do one last thing for me: I need it to look after me in my next stage, whatever I decide to do.

For the business to play its part, I need to make sure that the plan is right; I think I'm owed. You are too – you too can have payback for all your hard work. Let's start the journey by thinking about how doing something as radical as this will affect everyone, including you. Then work out a plan to get your business and yourself ready for a sale. Remember: you can jump off at any time; just because you're reading a book about retiring doesn't mean you have to retire. Just because you're setting up your business to sell, you don't have to sell it. You are in control, just like you've always been.

Your options

You are about to embark on a very practical journey which will take you through the twists and turns of considering your next move. Will you sell your business? Will you retire? Is retirement the best option for you personally? (It doesn't suit everyone.) What do we mean by retirement? I prefer to use the phrase *next stage*, as it is a cover-all for what happens next. When I use the word *retirement*, I mean getting out of what I am currently doing on a day-to-day basis so that I can concentrate on the next thing I want to do, such as writing this book. You will have your own version.

You may, for example, think that you are too young to be considering any sort of retirement and you may be right, but I believe that you are never too young to think about your retirement. The government have allocated plenty of funds just recently, with the pension reforms of 2014 making sure that we all start to think about our retirement years from age 22.

Only you can decide whether retirement is right for you, whatever your age. Do you dream of warmer climates, long beaches, sipping cool drinks, smiling and relaxed? That could be your life just around the corner. Do you want to spend more time on your hobbies and interests, start volunteering or get more involved in your community? Do you have younger family that you want to spend more time with?

I recently spoke to a businessman who told me that his greatest wish in retirement was to be able to afford to take his grandchildren on holiday. 'How many have you got?' I asked. 'None at the moment; my kids are nine and 13 and I am hoping that one day I will be able to do that. I know it's a long way off...'

What a brilliant goal, and he has plenty of time to achieve it. He didn't feel too young to be talking about retirement or grandkids. (Not sure what his children would say though if they had heard him!) He has a loose plan for the future and that's a great place to start. For him, the next stage doesn't involve travel, beaches and cool drinks; it's more practical and pertinent to his situation.

Getting out of the rat race is very different when it was you who set the rat running. Business owners involved in the excitement of set-up often overlook planning for exit. One business owner I spoke to said that they would be leaving the office in a wooden box (so no obvious plans for retirement there then!). Is that fair on the ones left behind? How will the business be managed in their absence? Even if you decide not to leave your business, I think that there are some useful exercises in the Workbook to prepare your business for its next stage without you.

Many people leave retirement, or taking it a bit easier, too late and end up being forced out of their business due to ill-health or other commitments. Unfortunately, we're unable to predict what will happen to us next, but we can ensure that as many 'what-ifs' as possible are covered in case things come around sooner than expected. Maybe in the olden days you would call this a key person plan: planning for an eventuality when the key person was no longer there. Perhaps after reading this book you will stay in your business but have a key person plan in place.

How this book works

The book is divided into five phases. In the first one we start by thinking about your retirement, selling your business and what that might look like. Next, we look at how to get the best possible price when selling your business by making sure everything is ready. In the third phase we take a look at the numbers, starting with your business numbers as we continue to prepare your business for sale. Our attention is then turned to your personal financial situation. You will be able to answer questions like: 'How much will I need to retire and during retirement?'

We move on to look at the systems you'll need to put in place to achieve your next-stage goals. Finally, you are encouraged to decide, after having read through the book, whether to retire or not, or whether to sell your business or not. To help you make sense of all of this and to get you really thinking about your options, download the free Workbook which accompanies this book. It guides you through your own thinking, providing a personalized, private written record which you can look back on at any time. Complete the Workbook as you go along or dip in and out of it to help you come to your decision. Find it at terribourne.com.

Phase One

Analysing your options

Introduction

In this first phase you are encouraged to assess your individual situation. It would be impossible for me to give you a blueprint to work from, or a 'one-size-fits-all' solution. This phase gives you tools to work with to find your starting point; you can then move on from there. The Workbook which accompanies this book will become invaluable as you jot down your responses to the questions you need to ask yourself.

Chapter One

Key questions to consider

Welcome to *The Beginning of the End* and congratulations on thinking about your retirement options before you have to (which I assume is why you are here). When we think of retirement, we conjure up images of people older than us, but you don't have to wait until you are old to retire. If you follow the steps in this book, you may realize that you too could retire, in one way or another. You don't have to be old; you don't have to wait until a pre-ordained age; you don't even have to give up your work or business status.

The world of work is changing as more people are choosing to, or need to, work beyond their official retirement age. In May 2019, *The Guardian* pointed to data from the Office for National Statistics, which reported that nearly half a million people over 70 years of age are still working (an increase of 135% since

2009).[1] This means that almost one in 12 people are working into and beyond their seventies. Is that what you want?

Chapter One is designed to help you clarify whether or not you are ready to retire. You are the focus for your retirement. We all know our given retirement age (mine has gone up seven years recently) but that doesn't mean that we have to go along with it. That's just an expectation. Someone else's expectation.

By the end of this chapter you should be in a position to decide whether retirement could be an option for you and, if so, what you will need to think about and do in order to achieve the retirement you want. Ask yourself these five questions:

- How will it affect my well-being?
- What's in it for me?
- What could I do next?
- Who is involved and/or affected?
- When could this happen?

---

[1] Amelia Hill, 'Number of over-70s still in work more than doubles in a decade'. *The Guardian*, May 2019. Available from: www.theguardian.com/money/2019/may/27/number-of-over-70s-still-in-work-more-than-doubles-in-a-decade [accessed 5 March 2020].

Start thinking about your next life stage, even if it's a while off yet, as planning is key.

Thinking explained

When I first started to look at business retirement, I realized that there is a lot more involved for a business owner than if you work for a corporation or local authority. In a 'day job', an HR department will probably contact you – or you them – to discuss your retirement options. This will happen at a certain time in your life, probably just before your retirement age. In a business of your own, where you are the leader of that business, there is less likely to be anyone suggesting you retire at a certain age.

In fact, people and businesses often rely so heavily on the managing director that everyone gets into a cold sweat when he or she tries to broach the subject of retirement. There is a huge amount of pressure to stay around, running things just the way they are – and that pressure could be coming from you! There, I've said it; it's out and it's OK. It's OK not to want to retire as long as you are the best person to run the business to keep it moving forward (I'll leave that one with you!).

That's what the first phase is all about – thinking about and facing those difficult decisions for yourself and for your business.

Most of our day is spent on autopilot. We do things automatically without really thinking about them and we have thousands of thoughts per day, from difficult multi-layered thoughts to simple things like 'where did I put my glasses?' (Check on top of your head!) The first part of the process of thinking about retirement requires you to think deeply about some of the questions put forward in the introduction. I'm not suggesting that you go into meditation mode but the more you can relax into your thoughts the better the outcomes will be. As you are dealing with private, and sometimes tricky, thoughts, it may be best to consider some of these exercises away from the workplace. You need to be able to concentrate, as you are about to consider how your next stage may impact on those around you, as well as the business itself.

When I am at work I often sit very still and just think. My staff, aware that I am thinking, leave me to it and come back in a few minutes. I don't close my eyes or lie down; I just sit quietly and concentrate. I will do this when I have an important issue to think about at work or about work. However, if I was considering options for my next stage, I don't think being at the workplace would be appropriate to allow me to think freely. You will need a clear head to tackle some of the thoughts in this first stage, so clear your mind and let's begin.

In order to get you thinking about leaving or retiring from your small business, I want you to consider five separate areas, which I have called the Five Key Questions. Each area is different but together they will help you to think about you and your personal circumstances, how you view your business and your innermost thoughts about why you may not want to run your business any more. For some of you, this may be the first time that you have been able to concentrate fully on you – not the business, not the staff or customers – just you.

Five Key Questions to consider

How will it affect my well-being?

Is there a reason why you picked up this book today? Did something happen at work? Do you feel overwhelmed by the responsibility? Did you meet a contemporary who is 'living the dream', retired and loving it? Did you hear about someone's illness or death? Or perhaps you've got your eye on something you'd like to spend more time on. There may be many and varied reasons for you to be interested in a book which guides you through the thinking part of your next life stage.

What started me thinking about retirement was a feeling of lack of control. In one of my businesses we had some partners who we worked alongside. Because of the fragile relationship between us, they basically called the shots. I used examples of their bad behaviours and poor management skills to train my staff and others, as they gave me plenty of examples of how not to behave. As a business we had to put up with some of their shortcomings in order to keep that business ticking over. Most of the time this was do-able but just occasionally it all got on top of me and I'd think: 'Right, that's it. I'm giving it up. Why should I have to deal with this?'

I know it sounds irrational, and where would I have been without my supply of poor management skills to find teaching and learning points for my colleagues! However, there was no 'give' from them; they just took and occasionally that became an issue for me. As a result of this feeling, and the overwhelming feeling of powerlessness and constant battles, I was in talks with agencies to sell my business. But I kept coming back to that not being a good idea. It was a good business, making a modest profit, which kept my family in work, so why would I give it up? The answer, of course, was stress.

Stress can affect us in many ways. I know from my own experience that the feelings described above were completely due to stress. I've worked out my own ways of dealing with this, and recognition was my first insight. I thought that I thrived on a bit of adrenaline: making me go faster and harder after my goals, etc. However, stress can also affect your health and well-being. Is this a good enough reason to give up your business and retire?

Stress is one of those factors which is great when it's working for you but can have devastating consequences when it works against you. We have all heard stories of the seemingly healthy senior executive or business owner who has had a stroke or nervous breakdown, or worse, in response to their stress levels at work.

According to Bupa (2018), 64% of business leaders are suffering from mental health problems, including anxiety, depression and stress, with work being cited as the main cause.[2] Josh Wilson writing in *The Telegraph* in November 2018, stated that work-related stress, anxiety or depression accounts for over half of all working days lost due to ill-health in Great Britain.[3] Unfortunately, as

---

[2] 'Two thirds of business leaders have suffered from mental health conditions', Bupa, 2018. Available from: www.bupa.com/newsroom/news/business-leaders-mental-health-study [accessed 5 March 2020].

[3] Josh Wilson, 'Work-related stress and mental illness now accounts for over half of work absences', *The Telegraph*, November 2018. Available from: www.telegraph.co.uk/news/2018/11/01/work-related-stress-mental-illness-now-accounts-half-work-absences [accessed 5 March 2020].

we all know, as an entrepreneur or business owner, you rarely feel able to take a day off from work, no matter what the cause or how unwell you are.

Your own current well-being and general health should be a consideration when you are thinking about retiring or your next stage. Similarly, you will need to consider your health going forward. Perhaps you have some illness or inherited condition which will affect you in the near future? Do you want to get a few things done before your health deteriorates?

For most people, they want to be in a position to enjoy the next stage after many years of hard work. In addition, many small business owners have faced personal sacrifices for the business, as I have, over their working years. Retirement can be payback time but only if you are fit enough to enjoy it. Don't leave it too late to think about what you want to do.

As the Spanish philosopher Baltasar Gracián said: 'Quit whilst you're ahead.'

From a well-being point of view, you need to consider your current health issues, ones that could affect you in the immediate future and ones that could affect you longer term (that you may be aware of). This information is important to help you make an informed decision about whether you are ready to move to your next stage or retire.

Use the Workbook (available at terribourne.com) to start to build up your thinking. The first question relates to what everyone else is doing. I know that I find it hard to hear about contemporaries, often younger than me, who have been able to retire. I also find it motivating. It is something to work towards, to make my retirement better, when I am ready. Use the experience of others to motivate you.

Working out what you don't like about your business will also help you to clarify your thoughts. Do you get annoyed or stressed by certain individuals, systems or clients? You may have to dig deep into your own private world to address these issues. For that reason, your Workbook should be absolutely confidential. By addressing these concerns, you may find that there are solutions which jump out at you. For example, if you hate doing the wages... outsource it! You don't have to wait to retire or sell your business to make changes. There would be a cost implication, but, after handing it over, if it makes you feel happier about your business, that has to be worth it.

Think about every scenario that you deal with. How do you react? Do some things make you feel stressed? Do you recognize your own stress? Does your stress affect others or the smooth running of the business? How do you feel about certain roles within your business, for you and others? Now think about how that could be changed. Don't worry at the moment about how you are going to do this or afford it. You can work that out later.

Lastly in this section of your Workbook, you need to think about your health. Stress may come into this, alongside any health concerns. There are, of course, unknown health conditions, but as we cannot know what the future holds for us, in terms of health or even death, there seems little point in adding this to our worry list. In the chapter on finance and getting your finances in order we look at contingencies for the unknown, so future unknown health problems can be thought about a bit later.

What's in it for me?

This is your opportunity to think and dream big. What would life be like for you if you didn't have to go into work each day? How would that make you feel? I suggest you get a pen and make some notes in your Workbook. You might surprise yourself with your scribblings if you let yourself truly think outside the box. At this stage, I don't want you to think about the money side of things or how you can afford to do what you want to do. This section is purely about how you will feel when your focus is not on work.

Continuing the theme from the last section, firstly, think about your stress levels. How could this change if you were no longer responsible for your business? Would you be able to cope with not having that type of responsibility?

Perhaps you are thinking that a change in career would be the best option for you? If so, what does this look like? How many hours do you anticipate working per week? Are you considering a new business altogether or an adjacent move from the one you already run?

'Textbook' business

In 2008 I set up a childcare voucher business. This was an adjacent move to my childcare business at a time when I was running 16 different sites. The voucher business helped parents save money through government-backed tax initiatives. Due to it being an online system, it was open to any parent using registered childcare and not just those parents who used our services. I still regard the voucher business as a 'textbook' business, as I applied all my hard-won knowledge into getting it going, and it was easy. I started with the end in mind and worked at the systems that the business would employ before even opening it up to the public. I had everything in place prior to marketing and it was all online. It was so much easier than setting up my main business, where I had sort of stumbled around over the years, particularly at the beginning, making mistakes and poor decisions as I went along.

Being able to apply all that experience and knowledge made business a pleasure and fun again. If you are thinking of moving out of your current business into another one, you may find that your stress levels are reduced. You are already experienced in terms of business pitfalls and what you would do differently if you restarted your own business. Of course, the thought of starting again in business may be very far removed from what you would regard as fun. That's OK too. It's all about exploring your options and at this stage they can be as wild or different as you want them to be. No one else need know what you are thinking.

Some questions to ask yourself

- What about a new start or a new work pattern?
- A different role within your organization?

- What do you really enjoy doing?
- What not so much?
- Why do you have to do it?
- Can someone else be trained to sort that out for you?
- How would it look for you if you were only doing what you really enjoyed doing?
- Would that make a difference to your well-being and stress levels?

In a discussion with a business friend about retiring from some of my roles and responsibilities, she said: 'You can't just do the finance because you like it.' Well, I've got news for you: you *can* do one aspect of your business if you change your role. It is do-able. You are in charge so can make decisions about exactly how your business is run, now and in the future. Don't get stuck in a rut thinking that you can only do what you've always done. As Albert Einstein said, the definition of insanity is expecting a different result from doing the same thing repeatedly. If you want your outcomes to be different – and I think that is why you are reading this book – then change of some sort is inevitable. Think *big*.

How would such a change affect relationships with your partner, your children, your parents and your friends? If you had more time to spend with the people that you care about, what would that look like? Time to let your mind wander to take full advantage of this option. You may have become a grandparent or have a parent that needs extra help. It might be that you would like to spend more time with a loved one and share some experiences – travel, for example. All of these changes are within your grasp. You need to allow yourself to dream as big and as outrageously as you like.

What could I do next?

This is the exciting bit. Time to think about what you would want to do next if you didn't have your business. This is a bit like dream building. Take to your Workbook and let it flow out of you. What is it you would like to do? There are no limits here, apart from your imagination, so if a trip to the moon is on your wish list then write it down. In the 'what next' section, we will concentrate on building up a physical picture of what your next stage will look like. Unlike the last section where you were concentrating on your feelings and how it would affect you, this section is about actual plans. Let's take your intended moon trip as an example. You don't need to factor in costs or time or training or anything like that, as this is a 'mind roam' around all the great things you might want to do next.

Where will you live? For some people, the idea of moving abroad is definitely on their wish list, or at least a little place for the odd weekend. What about not living abroad – just travelling and seeing various places? If you want it, write it down; you can decide later how much you want it, whether to keep it on your list and how you can achieve it. Nothing is unreasonable. Would paying off your mortgage and debts be high on your list? Many people want to do this as a priority and for peace of mind. Living debt-free can make you feel released and reduce your stress levels. Later, we concentrate on finance as a complete chapter but here and now it's about your dreams for finance; making it happen comes later.

Do you have hobbies that you could extend or have more time for? What about skills you have always wanted to learn? Now is your time.

'What next' in your Workbook is divided into two sections:

1. Finance and living

Finance means what you need (or want) to pay for. This isn't about how much you need per month as that is covered elsewhere in the book, but about paying off debts, giving money to others (children needing to step onto the property ladder?).

Living is where and how you are going to live. For example: 'I want to live in France in a chateau'; 'I want to extend my house'; 'I will travel each weekend to a different part of the UK'.

2. Keeping busy, goals and targets

Keeping busy is about what you will actually do with your time – for example: learn French so you can speak to the locals, join a choir, volunteer at a charity shop, spend time with grandchildren.

Goals and targets – this is where your moon trip comes in. I suppose you could see this as a bucket list of things you want to do.

Anything goes in this section so don't worry that it might seem unrealistic. You can look at the reality of some of your options later.

Who is involved and/or affected?

At the risk of stating the obvious, I'm going to say that this is not just about you. Unfortunately, as a small business owner, you are in a position of authority and responsibility (this may be why you are looking to get out?). People rely on you within your business and probably outside of it as well. In this section you are going to think about how any decision you make will affect them. It doesn't mean that you are going to change your mind but, having given it due consideration, you will feel better about any decisions you make.

The process is designed to ensure that you feel you have made the right decision, so that you can enjoy your next stage without any worry or guilt. Let's look at who is involved, starting with your business. Staff, colleagues, customers, clients, suppliers – you may have more, depending on your particular organization. I suggest you take each in turn and ask yourself a few questions with that particular audience in mind. Check out the Workbook for help with this. In the Workbook we use 'P' to stand for a person and 'G' to stand for a group. You are asked to actually name the person or group. By doing this, you have considered everyone.

Question 1.
How will P/G react when they know I am retiring?

This is about being aware of people's reactions; whether it's a supplier or your PA, they will have some sort of reaction to the news. How are you going to manage their concerns? Preparation is key here. You know your people and how they are likely to react, so by having the answers ready for them, fears will be alleviated.

Question 2.
How will this affect them in their work life?

This is quite important as, depending on your next choices, it could very much affect their work. Let's take a simple example. If you are a key holder but want P to take on this responsibility from now on, then P will need training. They may also need more money or an uplift in status for the responsibility. Thinking around what you are giving away in terms of your responsibilities may make some people react in a negative way. For example, 'Why should I do his job so he can sail around the world?' They will want to know what's in it for them. By having these answers ready and some 'give' as well, you may be able to persuade others to do different roles. Be prepared, however, for some to decide that they too want to finish working – after all, you are! So, what's your contingency for that?

Question 3.
What do I need to do to make this easier for them?

This is linked with the above scenario. If you can present a new job description to an employee which gives them more responsibility and therefore more money, most will be willing to make the change. This is not going to be a cheap process for you, particularly if you are looking at replacing your own roles with your current or new staff team. Similarly, you will need to consider your customers and how to make any transition easy for them. Don't give them anything to moan about. Change is good but a lot of people are worried when things are not the same and so complain anyway, even if they are getting a better deal.

Question 4.
What can I do now/soon to start that process?

This is the million-dollar question. I don't expect that you will finish this book and then go into your workplace to change everything. However, if you know your plan going forward, then each and every decision from now will have that plan in mind.

Many of the changes will be quite subtle, small and seemingly insignificant. For example, if you want to use less paper, you can start embracing cloud technology almost straightaway. This may support your next move without it being a huge change for those around you. For example, you may want to work remotely but still have access to all your files. Making sure that all your systems are in place to enable this is covered later in the book.

Deciding when to tell people at work will be your next dilemma. You don't want to unsettle anyone or upset the status quo, so this too needs careful thought. Do you need an announcement or something lower key? For example, you could begin talking about your retirement, which may be in 12 or 18 months, suggesting small changes to work towards this. You might have a longer-term plan, five years long or more. Only you will know your timetable.

Depending on the nature of your business, it may be better not to inform your colleagues. For some businesses it is the industry norm to sell a business confidentially. It doesn't mean that you don't consider your employees; you would just need to go about things in a slightly different way. You would also be on your own, as you would not be able to share information about your plans. This may cause stress and anxiety as you may feel that you are letting staff and customers down in order to get to where you want to be.

My advice and answer to this is if you have genuinely thought about 'looking after' everyone in your quest for your next step, then you will feel that you have done your best by everyone. Your responsibility to everyone stops there. If the new owner of your business decides to change everything on day one, there is nothing you can do about it, even if you were assured that they wouldn't.

Employees are automatically protected under the law of TUPE – Transfer of Undertakings (Protection of Employment) – so their jobs and current contracts are safe. This cannot, however, account for their happiness, but neither can you be held accountable.

Family and trusted friends

The second part of who is involved relates to your family. Although this is about your business, your family need to be kept in the loop. You will need to consider how any decision you make will affect your family. For example:

- Will your spouse want to give up their work at the same time?
- Will they be able to if the family income drops?
- Will your decisions around your own business affect where you live and how?
- Will any decision made now affect the short- or long-term future for other family members, i.e. children at university?

In the Workbook, when considering your family, you could choose to name individuals or regard them as a group. Your circumstances will dictate this.

Plus, you may need friends or family, or a trusted business mentor/outside colleague perhaps, to run your ideas past and to support you in what you want to achieve. Although final decisions will need to be made by you, it's a good idea to try to get as broad a view as possible to make sure that you are thinking about this from everyone's perspective. As I said right at the beginning of the section, you have a lot of responsibility and people are relying on you. Use the Workbook to help you to clarify who you need to think about.

When could this happen?

Timing is key. Deciding when to take action can make your plans go smoothly or can set people, customers, staff etc. against you right from the outset. Don't underestimate the power of the right time. *When* you actually start talking about your retirement will largely depend on who you have to tell, what their likely reaction will be and your current relationship with them, particularly concerning how it will affect them. You also need to think about the order in which you let this new information seep through.

Some personalities may regard themselves as being closer to you and therefore expect to be drawn into your confidence first. But this is not about them. It's about you. You are the one with the news of change and although you should be careful not to alienate anyone, you should also be clear that this decision is about you and your next stage.

Unless, as previously stated, your industry tends to keep business sales confidential, then honesty is usually the best policy, taking care to assess the views and concerns of others along the way. In the grand plan you will probably need to work out many smaller things which add up to the larger picture; timing the release of information is part of this.

Consider what is happening both in your business and at home to work out appropriate timing. If you are just about to move house, it may not be the best time to sell or retire from your business. However, if you need cash to help someone onto the property ladder then you might consider this a good time. Only you will know the personal and business circumstances that need to be considered.

When thinking about the timing of your retirement, you need to start at the end point and work backwards to the present. If the aim is to retire in two years (the end point) you will need to work out what you need to do and when to achieve this. In your Workbook you could draw a line and put markers for key events leading up to and from your retirement date. Think of it as an information campaign where you want your staff, clients and customers to know about something new, so you drip-feed them some information on a regular basis and according to your own criteria.

Also, it's a good idea to have an elevator pitch speech ready in case you get caught out before your reveal. This will help with your confidence. An elevator pitch is two or three sentences describing, in this case, your retirement plans to someone. The idea behind it is that you could quickly tell someone whilst you were in an elevator with them. It's a useful tool to get you thinking about how to put something important across succinctly. You can have a range of elevator pitches for different individuals. If someone guesses about your retirement before you have had time to consider everything, having an elevator pitch ready is a really useful tool.

Let's think about that right now. The scenario is that you have decided to retire from your business this time next year. This is because of a mixture of factors; for example, one of your main contracts comes to an end in eight months, a senior colleague, Joe, will be leaving the company at the end of next month and the business has a special anniversary in seven months' time. A colleague, Rae, seems to have got wind of the fact that you are retiring; she doesn't know when or how but thinks she knows something. Although she might not get your elevator pitch, because you have practised it you will feel confident talking around the issue.

You might say something like:

> That's very perceptive of you, Rae, as a matter of fact you are right. I was thinking about retirement but with Joe going soon and the Big Birthday coming up next year, there never seems to be a right time. I can't keep working like this forever but I'm sure you could all cope without me.

That's her cue to either support or not support you – either of which you have an answer for. If she supports you, say thank you and maybe it's time to give it some more thought (the door is now wide open for you to open up about retirement and start working on those conversations). If she is not supportive then you can listen to her fears and address these in planning for your retirement. Remember, she is only one voice and lots of people are afraid of change.

Conclusion

This first phase was all about setting you up to think about the implications of your next stage. The Five Key

Questions outlined in the Workbook are designed to help guide you through your thoughts. Although the Workbook is divided into five key areas, there may be some crossover between them. They are separated due to this being such a big task; it is important to see them as a whole moving forward.

As a business owner you are not beholden to someone else's expectations of you, or what you should do. By working through this chapter you have hopefully been able to think about the stress involved in your current role and how this affects your health and well-being. If you feel that this is an area for improvement, then maybe this is the nudge that will take you further into the book, learning how to prepare yourself for a less stressful life.

When looking at your situation, were you dreaming big? Did you come up with a new role or direction for yourself? Were you thinking about freedom? The Workbook should have helped clarify where you would like to be next and what you would like to be doing. Did you surprise yourself with what came out of the exercise?

With all those people to think about, you now see why you were advised to go into a quiet place, where you could be objective. At this early stage it's easy to start thinking about contingency for people and the business, finding solutions for your dilemmas. Timing is one of the crucial parts of the exercise; there is no rush. Your next stage may be a long way away or just around the corner; the timing is your call. You can see that to put any changes in place will require a good amount of careful planning. Luckily, that's also covered in this book.

This chapter was designed to get you thinking about the implications of any potential decision that you might be about to make.

Chapter takeaways

Consider your own well-being
- How will moving out of your business affect you?
- How will staying in your business affect you?

What will you get out of it?
- Retiring early?
- New work pattern?

What will happen next?
- Your future plans: personal and for the business

Who is, and needs to be involved?
- In your business and around it
- In your personal life and around it

When is this all going to happen?
- Timing and planning are key
- Considering others when thinking about the timing of your plans

Call to action

Follow the Five Key Questions steps and put yourself in the frame of mind to move your thinking forward so that you can move on to the next step.

Chapter Two

Factors influencing your decision to sell

Preparing to sell your business starts long before you call an agent for a valuation. There is a lot to do to get yourself and your business ready for sale. Some may ask: 'What is the point of "tidying up" your business when you are about to sell it?' Well, it's important to leave your business and anyone affected happy so that *you* feel happy about your decision to retire.

This chapter is about your frame of mind when thinking about the sticking or exciting points in your business. No one else will see this work and it's up to you to be as honest with yourself as possible to get the most out of it. After working through a series of searching areas for reflection, you will be guided through what your responses mean and where to go from there.

Reflections and responses

For most of you running a small business, you are probably fairly hands-on. You are the business: when customers call, they want to speak to you and want to deal with you. Being small actually makes your next stage much harder.

Redundancies

In one of my businesses I once had to make many redundancies. This was a new task for me and one which I was not prepared for. The process was fairly straightforward as there are certain rules and regulations that you can follow (thank you ACAS), but the reality was very different.

I knew my staff well. I knew that Laura's husband had just been laid off, I knew that Sarah and her boyfriend were just about to sign for their first house and I knew that David had already asked if there was any chance of an advance on his wages (again), so I guessed that things weren't all going smoothly financially in that family. Because of my knowledge I was aware that any employment decision made by me would really hurt individual staff. Because of the law and doing things fairly, you have no real choices, but I can confirm that making redundancies is one of the most difficult, stressful and upsetting business decisions I have had to make. Perhaps it wouldn't have been so bad if I didn't actually care about my team, or if my team was bigger so I would be a bit removed in a physical and emotional sense.

The reason I tell this tale is that when you're thinking about your own retirement, you have to put yourself into a position of power similar to that of making redundancies: choosing who is more valuable to your business and therefore must stay, and who must go. Thinking about your retirement can feel self-indulgent, unnecessary and a bit selfish. People may assume that you're all muddling along OK and that you will be transported out of the business in a wooden box. You do have to think about yourself when planning for retirement but that doesn't have to be exclusive – you can think of others as well.

In this chapter you will be encouraged to do two things: firstly, to allow yourself thinking time; and secondly, to ask yourself all manner of questions to see where your sticking points are. The main thing to keep in mind is that there is no rush. You don't need to make a decision by Wednesday; you don't have to come up with a plan in the next fortnight. This is your thinking stage and you need to take your time.

On the *Reflect and Response Sheet* in the Workbook, you'll see that there are many different questions to think about. Some of these will be irrelevant to you and your business; others may be missing. It is a working document and is private. There are two ways to use the Reflect and Response Sheet: some people use it as a base to answer the questions on the actual sheet or in a new notebook elsewhere; others just tick the questions to say that they have thought about them. As part of your thinking process, you'll probably come up with some questions of your own and possibly an action plan of what to investigate or find out about next, what to put in place next or explore.

The process is yours. The pace is yours. The answers are yours. You own this.

I suggest that you skim-read the Reflect and Response Sheet first before deciding what you are going to do with it. If you choose to make notes, I suggest you start a new notebook (physical or on your computer) just for your ideas and thoughts about planning your retirement. Needless to say, this is a private and confidential exercise. You will need to be honest with yourself about your business and expectations in order to do this part of the exercise and do yourself justice. You deserve to spend time looking at your own future – after all, you have spent time in your business looking after others' futures, whether they be employees or customers.

Allow yourself a bit of space to complete this exercise. Don't be fooled into thinking that you haven't got the time. If this is a priority, you will find the time. It doesn't have to be done in work hours or at work – perhaps it's best that it isn't, so you don't feel as if you are being watched. If this is not a priority, perhaps the time is not right for you to look at your next-stage options, but when will that time be? The fact that you've picked up this book means you are already curious about retiring. Think about *you* now, not the business, staff or customers. It's your time.

How does the Reflect and Response Sheet work?

The Reflect and Response Sheet has been designed as a very simple thinking tool and is part of your Workbook. Although these questions look harmless enough, they are designed to make you really think about your attitude to your business. This very private piece of work will probably not be shared with anyone as it is your innermost feelings about your business. Spoiler alert: It may not all be positive. You may find that you have quite negative feelings towards some part(s) of your business – this is normal.

The aim is to exorcise these feelings and bring them out. You may well find that what you thought was a sticking point is not actually too bad. Or you may be able to see quite clearly why you sometimes feel negative about certain aspects of your business, and be able to fix or get rid of these aspects.

On the Reflect and Response Sheet, there is space to add a score on the right-hand side, which can be used in any way you like – for example, you might use numbers. However, I suggest that you keep it simple, using a traffic light system and scoring in one of three colours: red, orange or green. If, when you have considered all aspects of the question you identify a sticking point for you in your business then flag it up in red. Use orange if you are currently working on this and green if there is no problem at all. Be honest. You wouldn't be reading a book about retirement and selling your business if every answer was green.

Confidentiality is super important for this task. It is your deepest opinion. Don't worry if it turns out to be mostly red. The next exercise is to put action plans in place to deal with your problem areas. This may involve temporary or permanent solutions, depending on whether and when you are going to sell your business.

Reflect and Response Sheet explanation

1. People I work with

I thought we'd start with a big one. In general, we tend to say (because it's good for business) that the people we work with are great, a brilliant bunch etc. – but are they?

All of them? You may need to break this one down into individual personalities. Who makes your life difficult? Who encourages the others (negatively) when you least want them to? Who is a difficult person to work alongside but is great at their job, so everyone puts up with them? Is that the same person who is great with the customers, all smiles and joy, then turns into some unpleasant grouch once the customer has gone and they are back with everyone else?

The reason we look at individuals is that they affect your business. Remember in Chapter One when we looked at well-being? Essentially, we are discussing that here again. Unpleasant people are difficult to work with, so sometimes it's easier to put up with their behaviours than to tackle them. If you think that by indicating you do have a problem staff member, the next stage will be to deal with it, then you're right – but it may not have to be you that deals with this. There are lots of ways to outsource your HR, so don't shy away from being truthful here just because you don't want to tackle something. Being honest at the beginning may lead you to think that this person (if there is one!) is actually harming your business. Now that's a big thought. If you have stuff to deal with here, flag it up in red. No more head in the sand.

2. People I work for

I can hear you shouting at me: 'I don't work for anyone; clue is in the name – business owner, entrepreneur, own business!'

However, I would beg to differ (you knew I would). There are a whole host of people you work for. I'm not talking about your family income here. I'm talking about customers, suppliers, associates, colleagues with business connections to you, your downward and upward supply chains. There may be people sharing your building and although you don't work for them per se, you would help out if one of their customers came to the wrong door – you'd take a message or parcel for your neighbours etc. Sometimes those relationships can be a bit one-sided, where you seem to do all the running. If that is the case, it needs flagging up here.

It may be that the people who work in these organizations are not nice, but you have to be nice to them. Again, I refer you to Chapter One, when you were looking at stress levels. Sometimes the stress is not worth it. We once had a customer who though it was OK to come in and abuse staff by shouting at them and making a scene. As a new business, we had very few customers and she knew it, so thought it was OK to treat people badly. She was raised as a red flag in my business and someone no one wanted to deal with, putting extra stress on me as the manager to cope with her. The solution was easy. We made a decision to 'sack the customer'. The result was a much happier staff and an easier life for me with less stress. The downside of course was that we lost the income from her custom. But others had seen her behaviour and we quickly drew in more customers once word was out that she had left. It turned out to be a win-win situation for us, even though at first it seemed unlikely. Be brave: look at who you work for – do any of them need sacking?

3. Travelling and commuting

I have put these together here, although you may separate them depending on your circumstances. I once saw a business for sale locally and followed it up with the agent as something to potentially buy. When I asked why the business was for sale, I was told that the owner lived quite far away. On further probing, the owner lived very far away, with a one hour five minute commute each day, each way. First thing in the morning was OK but after work (after the long hours that owners do), the traffic had built up and the journey was about half an hour longer. No wonder the business was for sale. Two and a half hours added on to a busy responsible day, every day, doesn't sound like fun and the owner had done this for 14 years. I think that's called stamina.

Sometimes your trip to work can be useful (podcasts, phone calls) so it may be that this can be seen as positive rather than negative. But only if you like travelling. If not, then this may be a red flag for you. This can also work the other way though. If you are very close to work (like when I had an office at home), you can find yourself always in business mode and never switching off. Similarly, if you're travelling around in your business, how does this impact on the other jobs that you have to do?

4. Getting up in the morning to go to work

Let me clarify. I'm not talking about whether you have an alarm clock set or a wake-up call. I'm referring to your mindset: your willingness to go into work, your excitement at the prospect. If you worked in a job and not for yourself, would you still work in that job? It's a big question which requires a bit of unpacking for you to get to the bottom of it. If you find it difficult to get motivated in the morning for work, if your get up and go has got up and gone, then you will need to flag this up as red.

There may be a simple solution; it may be that you find the solution as you complete these questions. What has taken your joy away? Obviously, no business, or job for that matter, will be as exciting as the first few weeks, months or years, when you are learning new things, but if your joy has gone, this needs to be addressed. By you. It could be that you are bored, tired or need new experiences, which you could find in the business if you look in the right place. So, there is a bit of soul-searching in this one.

5. Working hours

Again, I have put all the working time and hours into one section, although you may want to answer them separately, so that you can see exactly where, if need be, your sticking points are. Long hours and little free time seem to go with the territory for entrepreneurs, but should this be the case? If you are affected by these issues, they can impact on your own health and also on the business. You do not operate as effectively when you are tired, or stressed for that matter.

It may be that you think the number of hours equates to the quality you offer. Does it? There's a reason why large companies are offering mindfulness workshops to staff. They want them to perform better. This applies to you as well. Four hours of great productivity is much better than ten hours of mediocrity. It's about working smart.

That, and losing the guilt that goes with being seen to work fewer hours.

6. What happens when you are sick (or someone else is)?

This dilemma is one which faces most entrepreneurs. You want to set a good example to your workforce but if you are ill, you are ill, no? Well, no actually. I know from experience that even when I can hardly lift my head from the pillow in the morning, or having been through several operations, you still feel as if you need to be present in your business. You feel guilty for not being there and even guiltier if you are absent to look after someone else. If this is an area that bothers you, then you will need to look at it in a wider context later and red flag it. Don't worry if at the moment you can't see how this or anything else can be changed – we'll come to that.

7. Having thinking time

Just a quick revisit to thinking time, as I feel that it is so important for your own peace of mind and the development of your business. If you don't get any time to think, maybe you can red flag this to see what happens when you allow yourself just a few minutes a day to cogitate and let your thoughts sort it all out.

8. Your working environment

Firstly, I want you to think about the physical environment at your business. Is it warm? Are there many flights of stairs? (This could be your first green flag!) Is it easy to park? Are the other tenants in the building pleasant? Would you like to own your own building? Would you like to sell your own building and rent? What about the decor and style? Is it open plan or smaller spaces? Which would be best for what you do in the building? Is it safe?

Next I need you to think about the atmosphere in your workplace. Is it a pleasant place to work and visit? Do people feel comfortable? Is everyone else happy with the workplace or do they have niggles which maybe need addressing?

9. Financial issues

Do you make an acceptable living from your business? What is that? How does that compare with others in your sector? In your peer group? Does the business make ends meet each month or do you stumble hand to mouth sometimes? Why is that? What have you made big spends on; what do you need to cut back on? Red flag each item separately, as they may well be linked, for example to one particular department or person overspending. Do you have a contingency plan for finance; if not, can you get one? Does your business actually make a profit? Are you in control of any loans that you have with the business? Does the business owe you money? Do you often you go without (a wage, dividends, etc.) to make sure that the business is OK – recognize this? What are your financial red flags?

10. Your responsibilities

Another big area for you to contemplate. This is often the single hardest part of running your own business. You are responsible for everything.

With this area you need to break it down into manageable chunks, so I have divided your Reflect and Response Sheet into various responsibilities, which may or may not be exhaustive, depending on your business type. I know that one of my red-flag areas for responsibility is paying staff wages, which also fits into my section on exclusive responsibilities. I have already put in a lot of back-up to help me do this but often I am repeatedly asking for information, which I then need to pass on to the (outsourced) accountants, for them to process.

The timing is crucial, and it seems that no one else can understand this, probably because they are not directly responsible. In practice, it means that if I don't get information through at the right time, I cannot send the wages for processing, which would affect the pay date of everyone's wages. (See how important it is!) I do feel the heavy weight of responsibility for this but only because I am relying on others to pass on correct information. This would definitely be one of my red flags.

Are you overwhelmed with your responsibilities? This may be a red flag area in general or it could just be specific areas. And lastly you will need to think about what happens when you are not there – holiday times perhaps? How does your business cope? How do you cope? Are there any red flags here?

So now you have lots to think about. Having gathered up all your red flags, you may start to notice patterns. Well done if you followed that task through. It was tough, wasn't it? But you should now have clarity around where your flash points are and how they affect you as an individual and your business.

The Reflect and Response Sheet

Now, look at each section or part of a question where you issued a red flag. Take note of whether these all relate to one broad subject, e.g. people or a particular person, or whether they relate to something else. You are looking for patterns to see if there is a common theme going through your private thoughts about your business.

No.	Areas for reflection	Score
1.	People I work with	
2.	People I work for	
3.	Travelling to work/commute	
	Travelling when at work/for business	
4.	Getting up in the morning to go to work	
5.	Working at weekends	
	Working longer than average days	
6.	What happens when you are sick (or someone else is?)	
7.	Having thinking time	
8.	Your working environment – the buildings	
	General work environment – the atmosphere	
9.	Financial issues – making ends meet each month for the business	
	Financial issues – making a profit	
	Financial issues – loans and other special payments	
	Making an acceptable living from your business	
10.	Your responsibilities– staff	
	Your responsibilities – paying bills and wages	
	Your responsibilities – health and safety	
	Your responsibilities – your specific role that no one else does	
	Your responsibilities – how do you feel about them in general?	
	Your responsibilities – who runs things when you are not there?	

When a business friend of mine followed this exercise, he found that he had flags in two places that were linked. He had flagged a certain person as being disagreeable and then he had flagged his own staffing responsibilities. In this part of the exercise it came to light that the two were connected. Basically, he didn't like dealing with this person himself and didn't enjoy working with them, which made him feel anxious about going into work. He also didn't like dealing with the stress of other staff members' complaints about this person. When he looked for patterns, it was there, coming at him from several different angles and it was all to do with one personality.

What next?

The purpose of the next exercise is to sort out some or all of these problem red flags. For this you will need to use an action plan. I've included a simple action plan in the Workbook, or you can use your own. I think you know how this works. The action plan should be easy to follow, be of benefit to sort out your problem and have a designated timeframe. There's no point in writing something down that you need to happen 'soon'; it needs to be by a certain day or time, so that you know when it is achieved.

Using these tools, you will be able to see the sticking points about your business. Remember: this part of the process is completely confidential. No one knows you are doing it or what you are doing. It might serve, however, to put a few things in perspective. It may not all be red flags; there could be green ones (beyond the walking up the stairs, keeping fit one!). Many could be orange, in that you have identified a problem but are already dealing with it. In this case, you need to write some action plans to ensure that the current solution that you are working on doesn't take too long.

You may end up with some hard-hitting action plans. It could be that you see clearly that you need to move office due to all the red flags, or that a customer is no longer positive for your business. Or that your business is moving in a different direction to your expectations. I'm sure you will find something and it's for your eyes and thoughts only. The exercise should, however, give you a better understanding of yourself and your attitude to your business.

Chapter takeaways

The questions you need to ask relate to:

- People inside and outside your business
- Travel, time management and environment
- The financial picture
- Your personal responsibilities within the business

Call to action

Work through the Reflect and Response Sheet.

Phase Two

Preparing to sell your business

Introduction

Having put your thoughts into perspective in Phase One, now you will look objectively at what it is you have for sale and how you can make this better. You are probably familiar with a SWOT analysis, so we use one here to help you to assess your business. This is for a prospective buyer, who will want to know everything. So you need to highlight the positives of your business despite any negative thoughts that have just been brought up by your question task.

At the end of the next chapter you will be one step closer to deciding whether selling your business is a good idea and to knowing the steps you need to put in place. By completing the SWOT exercise in the Workbook, you'll start to get all your information (except the finances, which comes in the next phase) in one place.

In addition, complete the *Sum Up Report* to give to any (serious) prospective buyer – this will outline your business in one place. The Sum Up Report doesn't contain your innermost secretive thoughts. Instead, it is a summary of the best bits about your business and is used as a business sales tool. Most of it can be completed by the end of this chapter, leaving just the financial picture to add when you have read through Phase Three.

Chapter Three

SWOT to sell

In this phase you are going to try to get your business ready for sale. One of the things that struck me about wanting to sell my business was how under-prepared I felt. This puts you on the back foot – the opposite of being in control, which is where you want to be. My personal feeling is that the more in control you feel, the more comfortable you will be about letting your business go. I am going to take you through something that you have probably done before: a SWOT analysis. But this time you will be concentrating on looking at how to sell your business. I have chosen a SWOT analysis as most people seem to understand the basic principles. For those who do, miss out the next paragraph.

SWOT stands for *strengths*, *weaknesses*, *opportunities* and *threats*, and relates to your business. The normal way to do a SWOT analysis is to divide a large square into four equal squares. You write one of the SWOT words in each of the smaller squares, being careful to make sure you have room to write underneath. You will find one in your Workbook. It looks like this:

Strengths	Weaknesses
Opportunities	Threats

The words apply to your business, so the strengths as you see them, your business weaknesses, opportunities (for more business, expansion, customers, etc.) and threats – these can be internal or external threats which may affect your business. And that's it.

So why use a SWOT analysis when thinking about selling a business?

- It's a tool that most business owners are familiar with, so there's no need to re-invent the wheel
- You don't need any specialist equipment
- It's easy to read and understand
- You can easily add or adjust information (particularly if you make it from a table in Word – or Pages for Mac users – like I did)

We'll go through each of the squares in turn, so that you get a full understanding of what you are doing in terms of your retirement. Treat this as a free-thinking exercise; don't over-analyse what you put into each box. You can prune out the negative stuff later. Don't worry, either, if you put a strength into the weaknesses box – this can be sorted out when you start to analyse what you have jotted down.

Strengths

All the best bits about your business. What makes it really good? What is your unique selling point (USP)? What is it that you have which no one else does? Or no one else does as well? Don't rush this process. You can probably write a few things down almost straightaway and others will come later. Keep a notepad handy to jot things down. Think of all the things that could be regarded as strengths, even if they are a bit tenuous. You can sort it out later. Put only one word or phrase on each line so that you end up with a list. The size of the list doesn't matter at this stage. Just keep adding.

Don't forget to open your mind as well. In one of my businesses, we give children an afternoon snack – something like a sandwich and a piece of fruit to keep them going until they get home. A competitor calls that 'Tea', so the parents think they are getting better value, as they get tea at one place and only a snack at another. But in actual fact the food is exactly the same.

Think about what you do as a norm, which others may decide is a benefit. In order to do a SWOT analysis for my business some years ago, I looked at competitor websites to see what they were offering. I discovered that they were making what I considered to be normal and part of the deal into a positive and generous add-on for the customer. From the customer point of view, they may compare the two and decide that one sounds better, so just be aware of this when you're completing your strengths. I have also seen adverts for staff which say things like 'free uniform'. In the businesses where staff need to wear uniform, we give this to them free because we want them to wear it. In other businesses this is seen as a perk.

Weaknesses

Good, hard-core honesty is required here. Remember it is for your eyes only at the moment. Further on, if you decide to sell, prospective buyers will see that you are an honest and open person who can be trusted in other areas. When this section is completed, you may be able to address some of the weaknesses before the sale of your business. If you decide not to sell, preparing action plans for your weaknesses will enhance your business. Don't be afraid to showcase your weaknesses: they can be a strength in another way, especially if you work out a solution for them prior to deciding what to do next.

This may be an opportunity for you to deal with some of your weaknesses. For example, in my childcare business, we had a staff member with a very poor attendance record. For any business, this is a weakness, but as we work to tight child-to-adult ratios in childcare, this weakness impacted on other staff and the business. By highlighting this as a weakness, I was able to look at the situation dispassionately, realizing that this person was impacting negatively on the business, not just in terms of staff cover but financially in terms of supply and negative staff morale. My two options were to a) do something about her absence in work or b) move her out of the business.

I knew that any prospective buyer would see her as a weakness and may even insist that she be removed from the business before any sale were to be considered. Also, in terms of being honest with prospective buyers, landing someone with a weak member of the team is not a good idea, even if they knew nothing about it beforehand. It would make you feel that you had not been open and honest with the buyer, which may affect your relationship with them, and subsequently your health. Certainly, for now, honesty is the best policy, especially as this is a private exercise. You and your conscience can decide later what to do about any issues this throws up, when you start to look at and analyse what you have written.

Opportunities

What would you do with this business if you weren't thinking about selling it? What is next in your plan?

What new technology could you apply? This is where you get to run wild with your imagination. You may be in a rut with this business, which is why you are considering selling or at least getting out. You need to look at it from a prospective purchaser's point of view.

What would be the opportunities for them to take up? How could they easily make the business more profitable? When you see adverts for businesses for sale, they often say things like 'easy opening hours', 'opportunity to extend opening hours' or something similar. This is because new buyers want a bit of excitement for themselves. They want to make a difference to your already good business by adding in something to extend the business and make it better.

At the moment, only you know where these opportunities lie. You know the business inside out; you know what works. For example, two years ago we needed to extend the premises to expand the business. I personally took responsibility for the new build, visiting showrooms for new buildings, having meetings and working out the financial return if we were to extend the premises, which was very favourable. As it turned out, we were able to accommodate more customers by using our existing site in a more creative way, without the need for an extension. If I were writing about opportunities, I would put the extension down, as it was financially lucrative and would be a good opportunity for someone to take the business forward, even though we didn't.

Threats

What is it that is a problem for your business? This is usually something a little more out of your control, such as a lease running out on the business and a landlord wanting to sell the property. Or your finance manager talking to you about other jobs she's interested in.

It may be really important to you to keep the same finance manager because you have known her for some time and have complete trust in her. However, for a new buyer there is no such relationship. They might even have their own staff member whom they trust and would want to bring with them into their new business. In order to turn this threat into an opportunity, her move out of your business should be seen as an opportunity for her and an opportunity for your business. It's a good business opportunity as you can bring someone new in and train them in the new way of working, ready for your retirement or business sale.

Also, you can never second-guess what people are going to do, and it would be too stressful to try to do this. Everyone, and I mean everyone, needs to look after themselves (including you). So why be surprised when a staff member wants to leave? In the case of our fictional finance manager, she may know that you're thinking of retiring and wants to get out of the business before it is taken over by someone else.

The trick here is to put everything down in the right space, a bit like a worry box. Then later you can work out how to minimize the threats – even turning them into opportunities. Some threats are industry-wide, so any prospective buyer would recognize them and recognize your honesty.

The point of the SWOT analysis is for you to take a good look at your business and recognize the good and bad points. You will tidy up this SWOT analysis at some point, to make it suitable to show a prospective buyer as part of your selling package – the Sum Up Report, covered later in this book.

Analysing your SWOT

Strengths

Firstly, start with the strengths. What is it that makes your business unique? What attributes will a prospective buyer be looking for?

A buyer will be attracted to a business that doesn't need the owner to survive. Let's just say that one again. Buyers are not interested in owners who do everything and know everything because they are not buying the owner; they are buying what is left when the owner leaves. If your business will not operate without you, or falters without you, then it definitely is not ready to sell.

In Phase Four, we will go through step-by-step systems which will help to remove you from your business in order to be free to start another business, sell your business or retire. When looking at the individual strengths you have listed, make a note of all the things that rely on you as the owner. This separate list will be invaluable as a starting point when you come to Phase Five. Similarly, look at who you are relying on in the business. You will need to look at job roles, making sure that you are recruiting to the role and not the person. This sounds a bit cold, particularly for a small business owner, who usually knows everyone personally. But, as stated earlier about everyone needing to look after themselves, you need to look after yourself. You don't need to be ruthless; you just need to put some good business practices in place, if they are not there already.

By taking personalities out of your business and stripping it back to the basics, you can see where you need to make changes and put new systems and people in place. In HR terms it's called 'human capital', a term I hated when I first came across it. However, having got used to the concept of human capital, I can see the benefit of de-personalizing each role in the business. It becomes about the job and not the staff member. It's also a great opportunity to look at job descriptions and job roles and work out what the business needs, rather than what it has.

Buyers are looking for profit. They need to know that your business is solvent. A prospective buyer will ask for your accounts and these will be sent off to their accountant for scrutiny. At the end of this chapter, we look at what to do with your SWOT analysis and how you can use it to assist your sale. In the Sum Up Report later, found in your Workbook, you will explain your finances and other parts of your business, before the questions are asked.

Every buyer is looking for a bargain. No one wants to pay too much for a business. They are in business just like you and it's up to you and your agent to convince them that your business is worth what you are asking (or close to that amount). By pre-empting potential questions, you make the decision to make an offer on your business easier for them. In addition, you will gain their trust with your honesty and hopefully they'll be impressed by your business's ability to be run with minimal input from you or designated staff. The new buyer has to imagine how they would be running the business. The last thing they want to do is to fill your boots on a daily basis. The easier it is to take over the better.

The strengths of your business are also your benefits. Remember in Chapter One where we looked at 'What's in it for me?' when looking at the Five Key Questions? A prospective buyer is also looking at the benefits of buying your business and will be comparing it to another business for sale that they have seen. Unless they are in a very good financial position, the chances are that they will only choose one of those businesses to buy. To make it yours, you have to present the benefits of owning and running your business. These come from your strengths in the SWOT analysis exercise.

In terms of strengths you will also need to look at what makes you different: for example, you might say that the commitment of your employees is one of your business strengths; but so might everyone who is selling their business. Can you back this up with metrics? Perhaps in your industry, staff churn is common and staff move regularly between businesses. If you have had staff in place for some time, state it. It is more secure for a prospective buyer to know that they don't have to start recruiting when they take over, particularly if roles are well defined and don't rely on the owner to keep everything running.

Next on strengths, make sure that you are not going over the same ground twice. It is important that you have the strengths section as the largest section, if you can, but not at the cost of repetition. A prospective buyer will spot this straightaway and will be annoyed that what looked like a lovely long list of strengths is actually a short list with different ways of saying the same thing. They will feel cheated and you will lose the credibility that you are trying to gain as an honest and open business person, trying to sell their business.

Also don't waste words in this section or any of the SWOT sections. Use phrases and short sentences or single words in your SWOT. The shorter the better, as this makes each point quick and easy to read. Anyone wanting further clarification or explanation (and we need to know they are a serious buyer before this is given) will get this as part of the Sum Up Report, but it is not for everyone's eyes.

Weaknesses

OK, so how honest have you been in this section? Don't forget that this is for your eyes only at the moment, so anything goes. It will be a cathartic experience for you to get all the business weaknesses down on paper. A bit like a rant but in short phrases and 'one-worders'. This is your opportunity to be honest and truthful to yourself and any prospective buyer (with a bit of pruning later).

Most people are afraid of showing weakness; they believe it will go against them when in fact it shows an openness – all too rare nowadays. I have had the pleasure of interviewing many (too many!) candidates for all sorts of jobs, but the one question that always comes up in one shape or another is about weaknesses. From an employer's point of view, this is valuable for a few reasons: candidate honesty, candidates who know themselves, candidates who are willing to be humble and express humility, candidates who are teachable and trainable. As you can imagine, I have had many varied responses over the years ranging from (and this is the most common!), 'I don't think I have any weaknesses', to crass statements such as 'my only weakness is I work too hard, am too committed, care too much', etc. As their prospective employer, it's nice to hear that they are going to work really hard for you but disappointing that they can't find anything in themselves which could do with improvement.

I think the best way to view weaknesses is as opportunities for improvement. Nowadays, in interviews, I don't use the word weakness; instead I say, 'What would you like to improve?' This usually elicits a better response. From the candidate's point of view, it also shows them that we are happy to work with those willing to make improvements.

Once you have tidied up your weaknesses on the SWOT analysis and made sure there's no repetition, you need to look at each in turn and make notes on how you could improve them. Let's take an example: you have put staff retention as a weakness because in your industry this is a problem. Any new buyer looking at your industry will probably know this and so will appreciate that you are being honest about the issue. In your notebook, make notes about what you can do to improve this situation. We know that this example is an industry-wide problem, but it doesn't mean that you can't come up with some good ideas about how to alleviate it.

A plan will start to form about how to strengthen this weakness. Examples include having an open day for people to come and try out working in your company or advertising for part-time roles to make up a full-time role. Once you have done this, you need to look at each weakness in turn and change it into a potential improvement. You should end up with loads of notes on how you could improve the business. I know this is time-consuming and involves you micro-examining your business, but it will be worth it. You are in the unique position of knowing your business best. You don't have to carry out these plans; you are just looking at ways of improving the weaknesses.

A word of warning here: just because you tried something once some time ago and it didn't work doesn't mean it will not work again. If I have heard that excuse once, I have heard it a thousand times. We've tried that and it doesn't work, the customers didn't like it, the staff thought it was a bad idea. What I say to that is which customers didn't like it – the ones who have long since left us, similarly with employees? The nature of any business is that it is constantly evolving, so how can we pick a point in the future and decide that something we tried three years ago won't work? The business, customers, workers, systems – everything probably – has changed so the new idea may now work. It's often used as an excuse to be lazy or to be negative for the sake of it. Businesses change, opportunities for improvement change, people change. Thankfully, everything changes. So, don't be pulled into the trap of others (or yourself) thinking that because you have tried something once and it didn't work that time, under those circumstances, that it won't work now or in the future. Remember Thomas Edison and his light bulb.

Opportunities

Here you can let your imagination run wild. What would you do if you still wanted to keep the business? What is on the horizon? How you quantify this is important. For any prospective buyer, you are showing them that this business still has lots to offer. A new buyer will want to put their own stamp on any new venture. They may have been attracted to your business because it fits with what they are already doing, or they can see the potential in it.

Buyers are going to want to see which opportunities they can take up to improve your business and make it even more successful (and this may not be just about the numbers). What opportunity do you know about that they can use? How can they use it or get involved? What would have been your next step had you kept the business?

This is the carrot on the end of the stick. The new buyer has already made great strides towards wanting to buy your business; now is the time to offer them a little bit more. A few prizes if you like: a goodie bag to go home with. A prospective buyer will probably spend more time thinking about how they can improve your business and take advantage of opportunities than looking at the finances, as the finances are being dealt with by other professionals. An entrepreneur will be the one looking at how to make your business their own with the minimum effort. Give them some starters, get them excited about future possibilities; this is what will hook them into making an offer and into securing a sale.

Threats

What external threats are there to your business? How can you mitigate against these? You need to think outside the box. Make notes on how to improve any business situation. You don't want a prospective purchaser to think that any threats are large enough to stop a sale. So, although you perhaps can't eliminate most threats, you can mitigate against them. You have been running the business with these threats so far, so it can't be that the business will not sell because of them.

For example, customers unable to pay is quite a threat to your business and may require a longer-term strategy. This is where you need to think about it. By thinking outside the box, you see things differently, so a threat that seemed mountainous and unmovable can be dealt with. There is probably a way to mitigate. A new competitor in the area is quite a threat to a business, or is it? If this was one of your threats, you would need to mitigate against it.

Competitor threat

A few years ago, a new competitor arrived very close to us. At first sight this was a worry. I decided to go and see them to introduce myself. This was for a couple of reasons: 1) to show I wasn't intimidated by them; and 2) to look at what they were offering, to judge its competitiveness against my own business, to see if there was a need to worry. It was an interesting exercise.

Firstly, they welcomed my visit. As a new business in the area they were happy to 'make friends' and of course they had heard of our business as it was so local. Secondly, whilst I was there, I saw an ex-employee member on their team, so already we had something in common. Thirdly, their business offer was not like ours in customer base, so I felt that the threat to our business was minimal. Fourthly, we started to share training opportunities for staff, which saved us both money.

Although something might seem like a threat, sometimes it is no more than an improvement that can be made, which you hadn't seen. You have to have the confidence to face potential threats head-on and embrace them. Having the confidence in what my business was offering compared to theirs almost eliminated the threat and worry completely.

Conclusion

So hopefully, after having completed your SWOT analysis, you have come up with some areas that need work or adjustment. Here you can either do more action plans for certain areas or put together a one to two-year plan with SMART goals (found in your Workbook) to mitigate against some of the more negative traits of your business. Honesty is the best policy. Don't be afraid to show your weaknesses and threats. It just takes a little imagination to turn these into new strengths and opportunities in progress.

When you have tidied up your SWOT analysis (so that you are happy for others to read it), it will be ready to be included in your Sum Up Report to be sent to any prospective new buyer, along with a SWOT explanation, clearly describing the points you make, so that no one is in any doubt. If you want to, you could include a sample one to two-year plan or some action plans for the way forward. If you were buying a business, how pleased would you be if all of this came to you, so that you could start to dream about whether this business is right for you?

Of course, it's an effort. Sure, it's time-consuming, but let's go back a little to the beginning of this book. Your aim is to leave your business positively so that you have no regrets. You also want the best possible price so that you can move on to your next stage. By presenting an honest report and explaining things to a prospective buyer, you are being open, honest and trustworthy. Who could ask for more? It's nice doing business with you!

You move on and your business is in safe hands because that's exactly how you left it – with plans for its growth and continuation. In the next phase we look at the numbers in your business. But first, we need to sum up exactly what it is that you want a buyer to know. The Sum Up Report found in your Workbook will be your selling tool for anyone who is serious about buying your business. It may even serve to create some competition between and amongst potential buyers. (That can happen you know!)

Chapter takeaways

Your SWOT analysis

- Think about this from the buyer's perspective
- Come up with brilliant strengths (unusual if you can)

- Weaken your weaknesses
- Show off potential opportunities
- Regard potential threats with confidence
- Hook buyers in with future possibilities
- And most of all, make sure that there is no owner required

Call to action

Use your rough, private SWOT analysis and make it better for others to see. Explain what you mean. Go the extra mile and set out some plans to show how to mitigate against threats and weaknesses. Complete the Sum Up Report in the Workbook.

Phase Three

Assessing finances

Introduction

This phase is divided into two chapters: your business finance followed by your personal finance. Both are important to work out. From looking at your business finance, you will know the numbers and be able to make an approximate guess at the value of your business. From the personal finance section, you will be able to work out approximately how much you will need to retire.

Chapter Four

Business finance

We begin by looking at what you need to pass on about your business finances to a prospective purchaser. Starting with audited and unaudited accounts, we then move on to an explanation of normal and unusual costs. The first part of this chapter concludes with a small section on TUPE – Transfer of Undertakings (Protection of Employment) – and finally, business valuation.

There is much to think about from the financial perspective when putting your business up for sale. By working through the general areas, you will gain a better understanding. Please remember that any comments in this book are not advice. I am not qualified to give that. Instead, they are pointers for you to go and seek professional advice if you wish to investigate an idea further.

Areas for consideration:

- The audited books
- The unaudited books
- Usual and unusual costs and expenses

- Workforce
- Business valuation

The audited books

This refers to the accounts prepared by a professional on your behalf to send off to HMRC. A good accountant is crucial to make sure that you are accessing all of your tax advantages, and also to keep you compliant and legal, if you have a limited company. Prospective buyers are keen to see 'the books' and the agent will ask you to pass them on for others to see. If you know you are going to sell (or are thinking about selling) your business, there are a few ways to prepare in terms of the audited accounts.

1. Speak to your accountant and let them know your plans. He or she is in a good position to advise you on valuation of your business and what to do in order to maximize that valuation. It may be that you have been overspending in an area or even underspending. It may be that profit is better than turnover or the other way around. Large business expenses, for example a new roof, could either wait until you have sold the business or, if you have it done, be a selling point for the business. Your accountant will advise you on the

best way to present your business through the audited accounts.

2. Speak to a few agents as well. They sell businesses every day and, again, are in a good position to advise you about what buyers are looking for in your audited books. In some industries, even a failing business is a great opportunity. So even if your books don't reflect your best year, you may still have a sellable business.

3. Get an understanding of your audited accounts so that you can answer any questions on them. If you are unsure of something, ask; nobody minds you asking questions. When prospective buyers or their representatives take a look at your books, they will probably come back with questions. Further on in this chapter you will look at answering the questions before you are asked them, giving you confidence in dealing with buyers even if this is through the agent.

4. Go through them for yourself and put yourself in a buyer's position. What would you ask about? Is there anything that doesn't make sense, or have you made a big spend in any specific area? Make notes for yourself in case you are asked about these things. Being prepared is key.

The unaudited books

These are your management accounts: the targets and goals you set for the business and how close you are to achieving them. If you do not have audited accounts, then a prospective buyer will want to see evidence that you are clear on your numbers over a period of time. For example, if you can show your predicted management accounts for a past period and how your actual numbers fitted into this, then this will give a new buyer confidence in your figures.

All of us have management accounts but sometimes they are not presented in a clear format for anyone else to see. This is an opportunity to put this right so that your management accounts look professional. When I say that we all have these accounts, most entrepreneurs are clear on their numbers and what they need to do in order to a) break even and b) make a profit. We wouldn't be in business if we were not making any money but I am also speaking here about predictions for costs and expenses, as opposed to income generated.

You may break this down into separate, general items, for example, as in audited books. This will highlight your professionalism and knowledge of your business. In truth, some prospective buyers don't get beyond this stage, so it's crucial to present your numbers in their best light. Your business valuation is based on the figures generated (audited and unaudited), so the easier to understand the better.

A business in good financial shape will sell quicker and easier than one which is not. That's not to say that you can't sell an unprofitable business (this may be why you want to sell), but a buyer will be bargain hunting if that is the case. It will be obvious from either audited or unaudited accounts if you are selling a business due to it not being viable. Buyers and their agents can be very shrewd. To re-iterate: it's all about being honest and up-front; then buyers can take a view.

Usual and unusual costs and expenses

In Phase Four we look at making sure your business is systemized, where possible, to make it easy for the next buyer and your next stage. Part of this is documenting what regular expenses you have: goods and services you regularly pay for and information on your direct debits and standing orders – see the Workbook.

However, for this part of the process, I want you to think about any unusual financial transactions. When someone is examining your accounts, they will ask questions: put yourself in a strong and open position by pre-empting them. If you can explain any unusual expenses before you are asked, then so much the better. For example, we had a large expense under maintenance one year, but this was explained by us having extensive and long-lasting work done to our exterior, including a complete repainting of the outside. This sort of information is important to a buyer, as they know they won't have this kind of expense again soon. Also, indirectly, it shows that you have looked after the building so far.

Another example was when someone was looking at selling their business. It was noted that the staffing costs were unusually high, with one particular person earning a very healthy management salary. When I asked about this, I found out that this person was about to leave in the next three months. When I asked if he would be replaced, I was told: not in the same way. The job had become largely redundant due to the recent employment of technology.

Moving forward, the company was going to employ someone part-time to check on the technology. This saving per month was enormous and due to the employee wanting to leave, the company did not have to consider redundancy options, which would have been a further company expense. You can see how clarifying the situation about the high wage-earner in this case served to alleviate any worries for a prospective buyer. By the time the business was sold, this person would have left and the new person on about 25% of his wage would have been trained and in post.

Workforce

If you employ people in your business, they have to be transferred over to a new buyer. This is the law known as TUPE. They must have no worse contract or conditions than previously, and they cannot be dismissed just because a new buyer doesn't want them. If your business includes staff, you will be asked to provide details of their contracts and wages prior to a business-buying decision being made.

I suggest you make a simple spreadsheet with:

- All your employees on it – you can anonymize it if you like by assigning numbers to protect identities (at this stage).
- Their hours – this will be on their contract, stating what their normal working week looks like.
- Full-time or part-time status – again, this will be on their contract but may help a buyer to ascertain why staffing costs are as they are.

- Their current age – due to minimum and living wage requirements. You may have a few apprentices who are on a low learning wage, but a buyer will see that they need to mitigate against their wage increase after training.
- Any qualifications, if relevant – in some businesses, staff qualifications are really important, which is why I have included it here.
- When they started with the company – this is important in case the new owners need to make redundancies in the future; people accrue years with the company not specific owners.
- Their wage and how often it is paid – so that a new buyer can clearly see the breakdown of wages compared to income.
- Whether they are part of your pension scheme.

You may want to give an explanation, as above, if there are any major changes coming up regarding staffing.

Tip:

If someone has said that they will be leaving, make sure that you have this is in writing from them. This will alleviate any confusion for the next owner and the member of staff.

Business valuation

How your business is valued differs from industry to industry. Some industries simply multiply profit to get a valuation, whereas others take the EBITDA and apply an industry multiple. Speaking to your accountant and the agent will give you an idea of what happens in your particular industry.

What is EBITDA?

EBITDA stands for earnings before interest, taxes, depreciation (of tangible assets) and amortization (of intangible assets). It is a way of looking at a business's operating performance and doesn't include factors like finance, tax and accountancy decisions. So, it's a bit like a raw business score. Different industries apply different multiples to your company EBITDA to get a valuation on the business. When the market is strong, you can make your 'multiplier number' bigger. For example, if the EBITDA of a company is £100,000 then applying a multiplier of 1.5 would value the business at £150,000.

How much can you sell your business for?

This appears to be the question on everyone's lips. In order to reach a valuation of your business, you will probably need to enlist the help of a commercial sales specialist.

They will be able to give you an acceptable figure in the current market. However, as a business owner, you need to beware of a few things with this method.

Similarities to selling a house

Firstly, commercial agents want to sell your business, as that is how their business operates. You may find you are told to put your business on the market for a surprisingly high sum. This is called a 'vanity valuation' and occurs when your business valuation is overpriced to get a sale contract. Think about houses and it's quite similar: the house on the street that goes up for sale at considerably more than others will wait a longer time to attract viewers and potential buyers than the one that is priced alongside similar ones.

Secondly, you will be given 'comparables' in your business trade for similar businesses that have sold. This again is standard practice to show you what is achievable, but actually until someone has signed on the dotted line, your business is not sold.

Thirdly, you need to be aware that the process could take a long time, so psychological preparation is key. In addition, you need to prepare financially. When a property is stuck and not selling, there is usually a decrease in price.

It's exactly the same for businesses. As a business owner you need to know where your limits are in terms of what you will let your business be sold for.

Fourthly, there is tax and other costs to pay. If you are lucky enough to get Entrepreneurs' Relief, the 'Taxman' will only want 10% of the sale price. The selling agent will want their cut for selling the business and advertising, usually 4–8%. You will need to engage an accountant to get your business ready for sale financially and to be able to claim your Entrepreneurs' Relief, plus your solicitor's fees, for the legal transaction.

You walk away with rather less than your asking price, less any outstanding loans on the business or premises, if you have any. You may only see 70–80% of your asking/selling price when everyone has taken their cut.

You need to research your business area for sales of similar businesses. You will need to be brutally honest with yourself to ensure you are not giving yourself an unrealistic valuation. It's hard when you have worked for a number of years in your business, building it up, to realize that it's not worth what you thought it was. Making these kinds of adjustments is mentally challenging as you may always feel that your business is worth more.

Working out the numbers on a fictitious sale

From the buyer's point of view

Let's say a business really similar to yours is on the market for £400,000 leasehold. You check it out and it looks like the profit has dropped a little in the last year (good – as this means an offer may be accepted). Be as realistic as you can and mentally make an offer that may be accepted by the vendor. Let's say you mentally make an offer of £375,000. You then realize that it's been on the market for over six months at the original price, so you try a cheeky £350,000. The vendor says no but is willing to sell for £365,000. You both agree.

From the vendor's point of view

Next, start to look at this from the vendor's point of view to see how much they will get for the business. First, we deduct 10% for Entrepreneurs' Relief; then we pay the agents – let's agree on 6% costs plus VAT. Then the solicitor's and accountant's fees (which may come later than the sale process – beware): let's call them 6% plus VAT as well.

So, we have £365,000 as the agreed selling price.

Entrepreneurs' Relief tax at 10% = £36,500

Agency fees of 6% + VAT = £26,280

Accountant's and solicitor's fees of 6% + VAT = £26,280

Total costs = £89,060

Grand total after costs = £275,940

So, what started out as an expected sale of £400,000 has actually given the vendor £275,000 or less than 70% of what they wanted. This is just an example and you may know of other costs to add in.

I encourage you to follow the above example a few times for different fictitious businesses for two reasons: firstly, to show that you don't always get what you want and secondly, if you don't always get what you want, what can you do about it?

The obvious answer is to up the price of the business to a price point where, even with deductions and costs, you will be satisfied with the outcome. For example, try to sell the above example business for £525,000, in order to achieve about £400,000. As I said before though, the market will not overpay, so it may be better to adjust your perceived value of the business.

If you decide that you really and absolutely cannot sell your business for less than a certain sum, for reasons which will be covered in the next chapter, then work this out and add on the costs. Decide for yourself whether someone else will pay this kind of money in the current market and up against other businesses. I have been through this process a few times and I never look at the selling figure; I always look at the perceived end figure, to see if this will sustain me in my next stage or if I need to think of another way.

When you have your end figure in our imaginary game, you then need to work out just how far this amount of money will take you and what you can do with it to ensure an income, if this is what you want. More about this in the next chapter.

The danger of vanity valuations

A vanity valuation is where a business is valued above its reasonable, achievable and expected price in order (usually) for the selling agent to secure a contract.

A business known to me has been on the market at what I regard as overpriced by about 30–40%. This business has been for sale, at the same price now, for about three years.

Q: Why is no one buying this business?

A: Because it's overpriced.

Q: Why doesn't the vendor reduce the price?

A: Because they have an overinflated view of what their business is worth.

A: Because they have made plans to spend all the money that they think the business is worth.

A: Because the true value (IMHO) is so far away from the asking price that the decrease is incomprehensible.

So here you have a stalemate situation where the agents have overinflated the price. The vendor believed the agent and possibly did not do their own due diligence as to an acceptable and comparable market value of businesses like theirs. They are now thinking that any decrease in price will be detrimental to their retirement plans, so they have been operating for a further three years with no obvious signs of selling to achieve their retirement goals. So, what has been achieved here with a vanity valuation?

- No sale of the business
- Possibly friction between the vendor and the agent as the business has not sold

- A disgruntled and concerned workforce, as they know the business is for sale
- A vendor who is in a business that she or he wants to sell but can't
- A retirement plan on hold
- A difficult job for the vendor, as mentally they have moved on but still need to work

Keeping an eye on what is for sale in your area is a good idea for many reasons.

1. You get to know what is for sale in your local area/business area.
2. You can start to work out a valuation for your own business, based on the valuation of others.
3. You can make a rough guess as to what your costs will be.
4. You can prepare mentally for the actual money in your back pocket.
5. You can work out whether the valuation will give you what you want in your next stage.
6. You will be able to recognize a vanity valuation.
7. You can work out where to pitch your asking price, in order to achieve what you want to achieve.
8. You get to know the agents who are actually selling, which gives you an indication of who to use to sell your own business.

Conclusion

As you can see, there is a lot you can do to help yourself and to understand the market a little, prior to going to an agent to sell your business. You do, however, need to make sure that you seek professional advice (and unfortunately that costs), so don't try to go it alone when selling your business, if that's what you choose to do. Later we look at not selling your business, finding different ways to work your business into your retirement instead.

You may get caught up with the 'dream' of retirement and what you can do with this lump sum of wealth from the business sale. Agents are great at letting you take up the 'retired position', i.e. planning for the future in your head, leading you towards making a decision to fulfil those dreams, which of course can be achieved if you sell your business and take your pot of money off into the sunset... Or, could you have it all? Could you keep an income and still achieve your retirement or next-phase goals and plans? Maybe you could. In the last phase, we look at making this a reality.

Chapter takeaways

Preparing your business for sale from a business point of view will involve the professionals. You can, however, make it less stressful for yourself by developing an understanding of the following:

- Your audited and unaudited accounts
- Usual and the more unusual costs and purchases within your business recently
- HR issues, particularly around contracts and TUPE
- Your business valuation

Call to action

Complete the Sum Up Report, including producing a staffing spreadsheet. Put your management accounts and thoughts into some sort of order for someone else to read.

Chapter Five

Personal finance

There is some work to do if you are keen to sell your business. In preparation, you need to know your personal business numbers. This includes what you take out of the business for yourself, or anyone else who would not be part of the business after the sale. You need to incorporate your expenses, your car, private pension, wages and dividends. This is your starting point to work out exactly how much you will need to live on, if you decide to retire.

The chapter is divided into four key parts to help you work out what you will need in order to move to the next stage of your life, whether that is retirement, selling your business or not.

Part One: Working out what you will need (depending on your lifestyle and age)

In my quest to research this book, I turned to Google (as you do!) and searched terms like *retire*, *retiring* and *retirement*. The burning question, albeit stated in many forms was: 'How much money will I need to live in retirement?' This came up with overwhelming regularity. It must, therefore, be very important to us.

There is no single answer to this question, as there are too many variables. I cannot, and neither can anyone else, say: 'Ah yes, retirement, you will need £100/£1000 per week for the rest of your life to live comfortably.' I can, however, point out the things you will need to consider for your own particular circumstances, so that you can work it out (ish) for yourself.

The main things that you need to consider are:

1. How long you will live
2. Health issues – known and unknown
3. Income requirements/expenses
4. Commitments – going into and during retirement
5. Contingency planning
6. Expectations – what are you expecting to do, i.e. travel the world, live abroad, buy a boat as a hobby?

1. How long you will live

Unfortunately, we are unable to predict this accurately, so we have to take a best guess. I am an eternal optimist, so for me I have a plan which takes me to the ripe old age of 95, with a contingency to 105, and then a different contingency beyond that (told you I was an optimist!). If I die at 60 or 65 then there is a contingency there to make sure that all my hard-earned pension provision goes to the people I want it to go to, e.g. my husband and children.

One of the most important things that you can do for your family is to make sorting out your finances as easy as possible. For that you will need to ensure you have made a will. I had one made when we first had children, to ensure that they would be beneficiaries in the event of my death and that of my husband. Things change over the years, so it's important to remember to change your will as things change in your life. Make it easy for everyone by making it clear what you would like to happen to your estate when you die.

2. Health issues – known and unknown

Alongside how long we are going to live comes the question of our health. The optimist in me says that I will be in excellent health until the day I die and therefore be in a position to spend my money as I wish. However, the practical part of me realizes this may not be possible and that I might need some of my pension provision to pay for carer fees, or a more suitable place to live if I cannot manage at home, or if other people cannot manage me.

I think it's important to think about this potential side of your life now whilst you are fit and able to share your thoughts and wishes with those who may have to make these decisions for you. And of course, this all costs money. In some cases, you cannot access services for your older age, for example, if you have a house or a savings pot.

You may know that you already have a health issue which will affect you in retirement, so can perhaps plan a little for this but you may need to add in complications. In addition, as we age, we may be less able to live independently so perhaps have to give up driving ourselves around. This takes out the cost of running a car from your expenses and adds in taxi fares, etc. The best you can therefore hope for is to plan for a healthy retirement, recognizing that your body will need some extra attention as you get older and this attention will cost you money.

3. Income requirements/expenses

During my research into exactly how much money you need in retirement, I have come across a variety of percentages and figures. Mostly, it is widely accepted that you don't need as much in retirement as you do when you are working and the factors that influence this are things like commuting, having a mortgage to pay, etc.

Reflecting on this, I think that those of you who are reading this book may be in a similar position to me. Having worked for a number of years on your business without taking breaks, building it to its present state in order to sell or withdraw from it, now is the time for you to enjoy the benefits of retirement or semi-retirement.

For me, I know that I have sacrificed lots over the years to ensure that everyone else got paid, the business was in good health, etc., so, for me, the money-required calculation is different. I don't want to give up 40% of my income as I retire. I want to have the time (at last) to spend my money and not to leave it waiting in the wings to rescue my business, if it is needed.

It therefore changes your perspective on how much is required and when. I have worked out that it will be when I first retire that I will need my highest income, in order to enjoy the fruits of my labour. I also recognize that I will need differing amounts at different times and that there are some payments I won't have to make, like a mortgage, perhaps.

4. Commitments – going into and during retirement

What commitments will you have in retirement? If you can, it is best to rid yourself of big commitments like mortgages before you retire. This is for many reasons. The obvious one being that you are not working and therefore bringing in a regular wage (although you are working towards a different regular income). Mortgage providers get sweaty palms when they don't see a regular wage coming in, even if you have a regularly paid pension. Also, do you want the expense of having a huge debt? Most people aim to clear their mortgage prior to retirement.

In addition, you will need to consider big issues, like changing your car – do you do this regularly? How will you meet the payments on a new car? Or will you be able to buy it from your savings? How much travelling or holidaying do you want to do? Any expensive items you have been longing to buy but not had the money or time to do so as yet? Then there are the normal living expenses. Household expenses may go up if you spend more time at home instead of at work (for example, heating bills).

5. Contingency planning

Contingency planning sort of speaks for itself and you can plan for a) planned contingencies and b) unplanned contingencies. The main aim of contingency planning is to give you confidence that you have some secret funds somewhere to call upon if you need to use them for something unexpected; for example, your car breaking down, your children needing a loan, wanting to move house. To ease spending worries, you will need to put an emergency fund in place.

6. Expectations

And lastly, your expectations and plans for this new time in your life. What do you want to do and who with?

One of the most exciting times in retirement is the planning of your newly found time. A plan is important for mental health. Some retirees find that they are at a loss without their business to keep them 'in the loop', making them feel they have no purpose. You will also need to think about your new identity and how to explain who you now are. Most of us identify with our jobs as an introduction to new people. (I run a childcare business, or I'm a haulage contractor.)

However, the main consideration in this section is how you can afford to do the things you want to do; how the plans you are about to make are catered for financially. There's a lot to consider as we decide our money requirements in retirement. Before we move on to working out how much you need exactly, remember there is no 'one size fits all'. You will need to consider the following: life length and your health, income required, as in commitments plus contingencies, your lifestyle expectations, and life plans.

Part Two: Working out what you already have in place

Let's start with what you already know. In this part, we discuss your state pension and any other pensions or forms of income that you could use in your retirement.

Government state pension

You know your age and therefore your predicted retirement age, according to the government. This can be found on a government website: www.gov.uk/check-state-pension. Just pop in your age and sex into the online calculator and it will give you your retirement age and date. This is important because when you reach state retirement age, the government pension will start to be paid, which of course offsets the amount of money you will need to put in to your income for yourself.

Your next job is to ensure that you have paid (or are paying) enough contributions to access the state pension. The tools on the government website will indicate exactly how much you can expect to receive. The amount is given per week, so if you are looking at an annual income, you will have to multiply this by 52. When I first looked at this, I automatically divided it by 12 to get a monthly income, expecting that this would come on the same date each month (my birthday day?).

However, this payment is made 13 times a year, once every four weeks rather than every month. At first, I was really pleased that I was getting 13 rather than 12 payments per year. Obviously, the actual amount is no different but for someone trying to work out their monthly income in the next phase of their life, 13 payments over 12 months is actually quite difficult to account for, as it comes on a different date each month, albeit on a regular day.

Finding out what day your pension will be paid may be important. You can work this out by looking at the last two digits of your National Insurance number; so if, for example, your last two digits are between 1 and 19 inclusive, your payment day will be a Monday. Therefore, bank holidays need to be taken into consideration, as you will be paid the following day if your payday is on a bank holiday.

I think it's really difficult to budget when some of your income comes through in this way, for example, setting up standing orders for bills and payments. If you are going to rely on the government pension to pay bills, you may have to consider using another bank account for bills that you top up by standing order every four weeks. Bills and payments can then be direct debited from the 'payments' account rather than your usual one.

If your aim is to make living in retirement as stress-free as possible, with a little thought beforehand you can set up bank accounts to work for you. All you need to do then is to set review dates to make sure you are crediting your 'payments' account with enough funds.

Looking at other forms of pension

When I first started looking at other forms of pension, I assumed that I had nothing, having opted out of my workplace pension into a private one in the 1980s. However, this was not the case. Prior to opting out, I was accruing a pension pot with my employer and when I opted back in a few years later, the pension restarted paying into my pension fund.

I cannot stress enough the importance of finding any pensions due to you. At the beginning of my journey checking on pensions and what I could expect as income at pensionable age, I came across a forgotten pension for myself. A chance remark from a friend made me question if I had accrued a pension pot all those years ago. She was coming up to her 60th birthday and was telling me that, although she had not worked for her employer for many years, her pension from them would start after her 60th birthday.

After a considerable amount of research, I discovered that I had a small pension from years ago that was still waiting to be taken. The pension I found, admittedly, is not a fortune; it's around £2000 a year, but it's index linked and will be paid every year until I die. Additionally, this pension starts when I am 60 years old, so needs to be added to my financial plan from then. I also discovered it will be paid on my birthday date, starting one month after my 60th birthday. So, although I cannot receive the government pension until I am 67, seven years earlier I get this workplace pension.

The moral of the story is to double check all your potential pension pots, in case they are active. You never know what you might find and every bit of pension you have accrued will add to your income. When it comes to deciding to retire, you may discover that you can put several small pensions together (from different employments over the years), making one larger pension pot under one provider. If you are a younger person reading this, my advice is to get involved in your company's pension scheme as soon as possible. If you currently run your own business, your company can make pension contributions to a registered provider on your behalf.

Part Three: Guarantees and index linking

It's important to look at what is actually guaranteed as income and what is not, as this obviously affects your future confidence in your income. For the most part, your government pension at state pension age is probably guaranteed. The only caveat here is if you have not paid enough into it, so now is the time to check this to make sure that you have paid enough in, in order to take it out.

You can use an online calculator at the government-run money advice service www.moneyadviceservice.org.uk/en/tools/pension-calculator, which will tell you how much you can expect to get and this is also index linked. Put simply, this means that it is likely to keep up with the rate of inflation so, in theory, you could buy the same basket of shopping for yourself at any time in the future and still be able to afford it. This is why it is important to understand which of your future payments are index linked.

For example, if you have a private pension and you buy an annuity with it, there is a vast difference in monthly pay-out if the annuity is index linked. This is because it is adjusted for future cost of living. Annuities are a bit out of favour at the moment, due to them not being able to give people the return on their pension investment that they require. Up until a few years ago, buying an annuity with your pension pot was the standard procedure at retirement age and exactly what your pension pot was for. Since the government White Paper, *Security in Retirement: Towards a New Pension System* (2006), people have been given more choice with their pensions.

As a rough guide, you are now able to do the following with your pension pot (although you would still need to speak to someone financially and independently qualified before making decisions around your pension, as these will affect your future income):

1. Take all of it out when you choose to retire. This is not, however, recommended as you will need to pay tax on the 75% that is not tax-free. In some cases, taking all your pension pot at once could put you into the highest tax bracket and leave you giving about 45% of your pension pot in tax. Not smart.

2. Take 25% of it as a tax-free lump sum. This can be in one go or at intervals. Lots of people do this to use the money to pay off outstanding debts, like their mortgages, and this could be part of your financial plan (see next section).

3. Buy an annuity with your pension pot and take a regular monthly income, with or without taking your tax-free lump sum first.

4. Draw down funds from your pension pot as and when you require them, or take it as a regular monthly amount, again with or without taking your tax-free sum first.

The above is a rough guide to what you can do with your private pension. If you are lucky enough to have a pension with a local authority, government department or a company where they have set up a workplace pension for you, then you will find that you will receive your pension at the age stated and it may even be index linked.

The age at which you can receive your pensions seems to vary depending on your current age and the different pension types you have, so you will need to think about these as well. For example, the new age for being able to take your pension is 55. This applies to anyone with a private pension. I have found out that my former company pension starts when I am aged 60. My personal, private pension, which I have been saving into as a business owner, starts at age 65 and my state pension will start when I am 67. On the face of it, it all looks a bit confusing. But with a little careful planning, you can account for each of your pensions and know exactly what you can achieve from each along the way.

I recommend that you start to think about any pensions you may have had over the years and track them down. Millions of pounds are lost in pension funds that people don't even know they have (like me, only £2000 per year but on my super-optimistic plan, I live to be 105, so that's an extra £90,000 in my pot and it's index linked). You will need to look systematically at all the jobs you have had and whether there was a pension involved. If you have always had your own business or worked for yourself and know that you haven't got a pension, then you may want to consider setting one up through your company.

Some pensions may not be guaranteed income. By this, I mean that you will find it difficult to predict what your income will be. This is why we start off with all the guaranteed income first and work from there, to ascertain what income we can expect. When we look at your financial plan in the next section, we start with guaranteed income, even if you don't get this until last (at age 67 for example).

Part Four: Have you made a financial plan?

So far, we have talked about private pensions, company pensions and your government pension. It's now time to look at any other potential income. Do you have other forms of income, for example, any property that you rent out, which provides a regular income, or another job/business that you can rely on? ISAs and other savings can also provide an income, for example a £20,000 ISA, which is the current tax-free limit, is a tax-efficient wrapper for your savings and could earn you £1000 per year, if it achieves 5% interest. I know that £1000 per year may not sound much, but like my little pension of £2000, it all goes to make a bigger pot.

In order to see your expected income when you retire, I suggest you make a spreadsheet similar to the one explained below or complete the example shown in the Workbook.

1. Open a new spreadsheet and put all your income down the side: for example, private pension expected, government pension and savings.
2. Across the top you will need to put your age, starting with the age at which you start to get your first pension, so in my case this is 60. I won't get any additional pension until I am 65,

when a private pension kicks in, so at that age that money is added in. Then, at 67, I qualify for my state pension, so another amount of money goes in this box.

3. When doing this it is easy to see where you will need the most money and then you can plan for this. Let me explain. Between the ages of 60 and 65 I will have just £2000 per year in pension (at the moment), so if I want to retire at 60, I will have quite a lot of income to make up per year to realize a healthy annual income.

4. Let's say that I am thinking of retiring at 60 from my business. This is where we need to make sure that the business value will support me during the years between 60 and 65, or longer if possible.

5. I think the best way to explain this is to give some concrete examples, so that you can see what you will need to do.

To do this, I am going to look at two different scenarios, which we will call Income 20 and Income 40, which is the annual amount that you are trying to achieve, bearing in mind that the income you aim for may change during your retirement years. As stated previously, Google seems to be telling us we require less in our older years than we do when we first retire. This makes perfect sense, as lots of people choose to spend time and money travelling etc. as soon as they retire, travelling and spending less as they get older.

Let's assume that you want and need 100% of your target income for the first ten years, 80% for the next ten years, 70% for the next ten years and beyond that. So, with that said, you can see how I have worked out the examples below. Other assumptions are that you have a private pension of £2000 per year, you have two full ISAs that return 5% per year and that your government pension is £8000 per year, with your retirement age being 67. All of these figures are used to provide an example only. Your circumstances will be different and will alter the figures, but you get the idea.

Income 20	100%	100%	100%	100%	80%	70%	70%	Need to sell business for:
Age	60	To 65	To 67	To 70	To 80	To 90	90+	Including all costs
Income required	20,000	20,000	20,000	20,000	16,000	14,000	14,000	
Private pension	2000	2000	2000	2000	2000	2000	2000	
Gov pension				8000	8000	8000	8000	
2 ISAs @ 5%	2000	2000	2000	2000	2000	2000	2000	
Total income	4000	4000	4000	12,000	12,000	12,000	12,000	
Shortfall	16,000	16,000	16,000	8000	4000	2000	2000	
Total shortfall		80,000	32,000	24,000	40,000	20,000	20,000	216,000

It is easy to see exactly how much income is required from your business sale if you choose to go down this route. The 'simple' version of the spreadsheet has you receiving an income from a pension of £2000 per year from the age of 60 (and ongoing), collecting your government pension at 67 and topping up your income to the desired level each year. It also shows what sort of money you need to clear when selling your business. So, for clarification, that's money in your back pocket after you have paid any tax, accountants, solicitors and agents.

Obviously, I don't know what kind of income you are used to or what you expect in retirement, hence working out the two different amounts. If this is not close to where you want to be, then you will need to double the examples or use the principles to work it out for yourself.

Let's do another example, using a target income of £40,000 to see how much we have to sell the business for. We use the same income as before.

As you can see, doubling our target income does not double what we need to sell the business for in order to achieve our goals. It's more complicated than that. At £856,000 clear for the sale, the business would need to sell for well in excess of £1 million when we factor in costs. You can play with these figures yourself to see how much you will need in retirement.

Income 40	100%	100%	100%	100%	80%	70%	70%	Need to sell business for:
Age	60	To 65	To 67	To 70	To 80	To 90	90+	Including all costs
Income required	40,000	40,000	40,000	40,000	32,000	28,000	28,000	
Private pension	2000	2000	2000	2000	2000	2000	2000	
Gov pension				8000	8000	8000	8000	
2 ISAs @ 5%	2000	2000	2000	2000	2000	2000	2000	
Total income	4000	4000	4000	12000	12000	12000	12000	
Shortfall	36,000	36,000	36,000	28,000	20,000	16,000	16,000	
Total shortfall		180,000	72,000	84,000	200,000	160,000	160,000	856,000

Clearing funds of £500,000 for the sale of your business

Target Income 20: As the business sold for £500,000 clear, there is £284,000 left over from the sale of the business to spend. This could equate to £7100 per year for 40 years, between the ages of 60 and 100, taking the target income to £27,100 per year. However, for Target Income 40, we can see that the money from the business selling at £500,000 runs out at about age 78, with a shortfall of £356,000.

Income 20	100%	100%	100%	100%	80%	70%	70%	Need to sell business for:
Age	60	To 65	To 67	To 70	To 80	To 90	90+	Including all costs
Income required	20,000	20,000	20,000	20,000	16,000	14,000	14,000	
Private pension	2000	2000	2000	2000	2000	2000	2000	
Gov pension				8000	8000	8000	8000	
2 ISAs @ 5%	2000	2000	2000	2000	2000	2000	2000	
Total income	4000	4000	4000	12,000	12,000	12,000	12,000	
Per annum	16,000	16,000	16,000	8000	4000	2000	2000	
Business income		80,000	32,000	24,000	40,000	20,000	20,000	216,000

Income 40	100%	100%	100%	100%	80%	70%	70%	Need to sell business for:
Age	60	To 65	To 67	To 70	To 80	To 90	90+	Including all costs
Income required	40,000	40,000	40,000	40,000	32,000	28,000	28,000	
Private pension	2000	2000	2000	2000	2000	2000	2000	
Gov pension				8000	8000	8000	8000	
2 ISAs @ 5%	2000	2000	2000	2000	2000	2000	2000	
Total income	4000	4000	4000	12,000	12,000	12,000	12,000	
Per annum	36,000	36,000	36,000	28,000	20,000	16,000	16,000	
Business income		180,000	72,000	84,000	−36,000	−160,000	−160,000	−356,000

If this were the case, there are a few things that you could consider:

- Reduce the annual required income or target income. (Target Income 34 or so works on these example figures.)
- Take less than 100% of your target income in the early years, therefore saving some of the income to take you beyond 78 years old. This may mean that you have to find additional income, for example, a job.
- Retire later.

There is plenty of scope for you to play around with the spreadsheet and make it fit your personal circumstances. Assuming that you have better potential to earn additional income earlier on, you could weight the finances that way on a new spreadsheet, so you are not worrying about your income as you age. It must be noted that if you live over 100 years old on any of these plans, your income will drop considerably. If you think that this will happen to you (and maybe you have nothing to sell, which is always an option), you will need to plan for this.

Disclaimer

My ramblings are in no way a blueprint for your personal retirement plan. I'm not a financial adviser, so am not qualified to give advice. I am simply showing you one way to work out your own individual circumstances and some of the things you need to consider. You will have noticed that my plans and spreadsheets are not index linked (I'm not that clever!) but I recognize that the figures and workings will be different in the future, which is why I advocate a decent contingency for such events.

Conclusion

We began this chapter by looking at what you think you might need for a comfortable financial retirement, linked to Chapter Four covering what you can achieve for your business. This depends on what you plan on doing, where you want to live and other factors. Looking at what you already have in place or expected, you were advised to make sure you know about any pension income and to take into consideration income due to you from the state pension.

Using a simple spreadsheet, you can set up a plan to help you decide if there is enough income for you, either from your business, your pensions or other income you may have.

Some of your income will be index linked and other income may not. It is important to know which will be, particularly when you are working out your own figures on the spreadsheets, and you will require an independent expert help you to do this, as it is tricky to predict.

Chapter takeaways

Find out:
- What pensions you have in place
- When they start
- How much they will give you
- Whether they are index linked

Call to action

Make your own personal financial plan spreadsheet.

Phase Four

Organizing your processes

Introduction

In this phase we look at putting it all together and making your business the best it can be so that you can sell it. One of the things we touched on earlier was that no one wants your job. They are not going to buy your business so that they can take over your job. They want to take over a business that already runs smoothly, so that they can add their own expertise and experience to make it even better. Most buyers want an easy time. So how can we make sure that everything is in place, ready for them when they take over?

At the end of this phase, and also in your Workbook, you will find the Three Folder System Map. The map also serves as a reminder and links to the System Revision

Sheet for the areas that you can and should systemize. I have deliberately left it quite sparse so that you can complete it with your own organizational structure.

Chapter Six

Streamlining your systems

Demystifying the business processes

I am keen to simplify and demystify all business processes to make things easier for the buyer. By looking at all the systems in your business individually and making sure that they are a) necessary, b) streamlined and c) clearly documented, you will be doing the buyer a huge favour. You will also be setting up the business to run smoothly when you are no longer there for your staff. Something to consider along the way is that leaving your business in good shape will make your journey on to the next phase more pleasant for you.

Some of you will have robust systems in place for some things but not others, so may find it beneficial to see how another business works. I have outlined the structured system that I use in my businesses. It was designed so that everyone, at all levels, could understand it. If your systems work for you, great – if it's not broken, don't fix it.

Finance, paperwork and people

In my own businesses, we keep everything as clear as possible. We only have three main folders: Finance, Paperwork and People. This chapter will guide you through most of the systems and paperwork you need in place under each heading to ensure that everything is covered. By following the Three Folder System, you will have a way of doing things that work for each area of the business.

It does take some thinking about. It may be that you are able to delegate some of the tasks to people better placed to document them, but it is useful, worthwhile time. It will mean that you can leave your business in a new buyer's hands knowing that everything is set to run smoothly. If they have a hitch or a problem, then they will find a document to sort it out, rather than telephoning you every few hours.

What is systemized planning?

Benjamin Franklin once said:

> 'If you fail to plan, you plan to fail'

> …and this sort of sums up systemized planning.

As a business owner who has been operating for some time, you will already have systems in place to help you run your business. To make your business more efficient, even if you end up not selling it, the simpler the system, the better. When business owners take a long hard look at their businesses – for example, when they are ready to sell and want the absolute best price for them – they often see things that are no longer necessary. Some aspects could be a throw-back to previous times ('we've always done it this way') and some plainly don't work. If you are able to involve your staff in helping with systemized planning then all the better, particularly if they are the ones dealing with these systems on a daily basis. Having a bit of a clear-out prior to selling is always a good idea. It makes you reassess all the bits of paper (online or actual paper) in your business, making for a tidier handover.

Which areas can be systemized?

I think it would be better to ask which cannot be or which are really difficult to systemize. The Three Folder System Map is a good start to see what areas of your business can be systemized. It's not an exhaustive list, so it may not have everything on it. Feel free to add more. Also, it's not a blueprint for systems, so some of the ideas may be irrelevant for your kind of business.

If you download the *Systems Revision Sheet*, you will be able to see at a glance which areas of your business you need to systemize and which systems you already have in place. You can make this as easy or complicated as you wish. I suggest you keep it simple and use a red–orange–green traffic light system, as you have done before, to give you a quick visual overview of where you need to spend your time.

The Office Handbook

In my business we have what is known as the *Office Handbook*. This lists all the systems and operations required to run the business and how to do them, step-by-step. It sounds like a lot of work, but it has meant that over the years, new staff have been able to pick up the job really quickly. As a manager, I don't need to be looking over their shoulder to check progress as it's all documented. The Office Handbook acts as a training manual or refresher course in all areas of the business. We update it immediately when something changes, so it is always up to date and, of course, it is cloud-based so it can be accessed from anywhere.

Tip:

You don't need to use in-house, bespoke systems for everything (or anything) but I suggest that you treat other systems in the same way. Let's take a fictional system called System A as an example. In your Office Handbook, you may have System A. The first item under System A is how to access it and the password, followed by some information about what you use it for. If this is a bespoke or in-house system, you will have the step-by-step, 'how to use it' guide next. However, if this is a system that you have downloaded or bought in, you may only need a hyperlink to the manufacturer's help pages. There's no point in re-inventing the wheel. If it's already done for you, use that.

Systems range from a simple email system to a complicated bank reconciliation system like Xero or Quick-Books. In my childcare business, we have a bespoke booking system for one department, where parents can book their child into sessions online at any time. In another childcare department, we use a commercial system to make sure that we know which children to expect, for which we pay a monthly fee. You probably have similar systems which are pertinent to your particular business. They should go into your online Office Handbook, so that there is access from anywhere, along with their passwords and 'how to' guides.

Doing the exercise above will enable you to see at a glance if your systems are fit for purpose or need something more. Be particularly mindful of only one person (you?) knowing all passwords, as this will ensure that you have to be present in the business, even if that's on the end of the phone, which you may not want. The real test of your Office Handbook clarity is when you give it to a new person to follow to get into a system you use and they operate it successfully. New staff are encouraged to add to the Office Handbook if a particular step is not clear.

External help and the Office Handbook

Whilst you are compiling your Office Handbook, make sure that you include the details of all external help, for example, the accountants, payroll company, maintenance staff or virtual assistants. The Office Handbook can also include people or companies you use less often, such as logo designers. If you make a comprehensive contacts list of who you prefer to use in the business, this will be very valuable to you and save a lot of time for staff, new and old. It'll also be really useful for the next owner.

Your business in a box

You end up with a business in a box. Everything you need to know to run your particular business. What a gift to pass on to a new buyer or what a gift to have within your business to run smoothly and consistently from now on. I think that consistency is the key. Whoever tries to work in your business will find this resource invaluable. It's bespoke to your business, having your name and ways of doing things written all over it. You know it works, as it is continually being tested and updated. Your business in a box should be in the cloud, somewhere safe. It's worth a lot to you.

Using the Three Folder System

As previously stated, I like everything to be simple to understand in my business. I like to simplify things so that everyone can follow them with ease. Before critically looking at my business systems, I had many, many folders on my computer. We even had folders labelled 'to be refiled'. It was difficult to keep up with which version was the most recent and therefore the one to use. So, we narrowed everything down into just three folders. These three folders contain everything (continuing the business in a box theme) and everything is online.

Within each of the three folders there are sub-folders, but only ones that are absolutely necessary. We have a map of the folders online as well, so if, for example, you want to find the tracking spreadsheet to see who has paid this week (or not!), then in our system you would go to the Finance folder, which is sub-divided into Accounts and Management. As tracking payments is a managing finance task, the payment tracker is in there. The fewer the folders, the easier the system is to use.

Below you will find a Map of the Three Folder System that we use in one of my businesses. You will be able to use this as your starting point alongside the example Systems Revision Sheet, which is also in your Workbook. By understanding the concept of what you are trying to achieve, which is to have a place for everything within your folder structures, you will be able to develop your own personalized bespoke system which links directly to your specific business. In the next chapter, I will walk you through the Three Folder System that we use so that you can develop your understanding in order to make your own folder system.

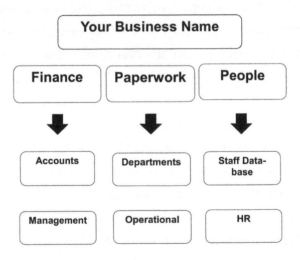

Figure 1. The Three Folder System Map

Conclusion

By keeping your business systems streamlined you will be reducing your workload. If systems are clear, documented and updated regularly, they act as a training manual for staff using the systems as well. This will of course take some planning, particularly if this is new to you. If within your business you develop an Office Handbook which covers all your systems, you are in effect creating a 'business in a box', ready and updated for if you decide to sell your business. Even if you don't sell your business, it is a very tidy way to keep your files, particularly using the Three Folder System.

Chapter takeaways

- Keep all your systems relevant and up to date
- Try to reduce all your business systems to fit them into a few folders online
- The Three Folder System incorporates Finance, Paperwork and People
- By having an Office Handbook you will have your business in a box ready for current or prospective staff or buyers to understand all your business systems

Call to action

Make sure that all your systems and procedures are necessary, streamlined and documented.

Chapter Seven

The Three Folder System

You will need to use your Workbook to help you get the most out of this chapter. Firstly, we talk through Finance and put in place systems to document all your financial transactions, in and out of the business. Moving on, the next folder looks at Paperwork, ensuring that all is in its correct place and up to date. Finally, we will look at People and how you handle your HR operations. The aim is to make the systems work for your business. Is there a logical order to everything? Can it be easily accessed and understood? In order to help you keep up with what needs to be systemized, you can access the Systems Revision Sheet in the Workbook. This will help you develop your own Systems Revision Sheet and Three Folder System Map specifically for your business.

The next three sections will help you to think about the procedures and systems you use in your business. You may want to document them in your Office Handbook. The main aim, however, of this chapter is to look for efficiency, efficient use of time, non-repetition of tasks and simplicity for everyone. Just because a system is simple doesn't mean it's easy, although we are looking for ease as well. Sounds good? Let's get started.

Folder One: Finance

Start with income

How does your money come in to you? Do you have a merchant account; can you accept payments by card over the phone? Do people make online payments? What about cash and cheques – are you still in the dark ages? You will need to take a long hard look at how your business is financed. You are looking for easy ways to improve what happens now and also to make it easier for people to pay you. It is really important that your money is trackable, and this may be an area for improvement. If you take cash (really?!), then you must have a foolproof way of collecting and documenting this to avoid problems.

Some years ago, we used to take cash on site in our business. This involved staff taking the cash from the customer and issuing a receipt. The cash was then stored until it was collected by a visiting manager and banked. The staff were taken away from their main duties due to sorting out cash payments from customers. As if that doesn't sound like enough difficulties, we also had theft.

Unfortunately, cash on the premises is a magnet for people who want to steal from you, even those who wouldn't normally steal. We have had one or two employees with ingenious ways to take money unnoticed, they thought, from the company. For example, by not issuing a receipt the staff member could pocket the cash. Unfortunately, the customer couldn't prove they had paid either, so in a few cases this caused problems for the customer and led to discovering the dishonesty.

One incident I remember was when a member of staff reported all the cash on site missing. Knowing that we had been 'watching' this person for some time, we went to see her to ask about the missing money. As we left, we suggested that she did a spring clean to see if she had put the money in a different place. We said we would return after the weekend to see if she had any luck in finding the cash.

When we returned after the weekend, she had 'found' the money and we were right: it had been hidden. She said she had forgotten that she had hidden it. We knew she had taken the money, but we gave her the opportunity to put it back and for it to be a mistake on her part. Result was a win-win. She didn't lose face and we still had the money. We learned a lot from this experience and immediately looked at our procedures for taking and storing cash.

The best option for you, your staff and probably your customers is to use systems which go from one account to another without the need for money to change hands. If you have cash on the premises it also puts you and your employees in a vulnerable position, which is avoidable. Spring cleaning the way that you take money in will also save you a lot of time. You are not handling cash or cheques and because everything is in your bank account, you can access it easily online and keep reconciliation in real time, making your cash flow forecasts easier.

So, before you write down in the Office Handbook exactly how people can pay you, make sure it's all streamlined first.

Loans and overdrafts

Make sure that all the paperwork, reference numbers and a spreadsheet of payments are all in your online Office Handbook. Make a note there too of who you spoke to and what the loan was for, dates and how much is still owing etc.

Outgoings – bills and services: how do you pay for them?

Look at all payments that you need to make. Can these be made online, by standing order or direct debit? If they can, then you only have to make sure there is money in the bank. In our bank accounts we have standing orders and direct debits for smaller amounts, as I know that the bank account will cover them. However, for larger payments like wages, rates and rent, I still keep these as direct payments as I know that I sometimes need to move money around to make payments.

It is a long-term aim (which I am still working towards) to have a financial cushion sufficient to allow all payments to go out of the bank directly at the appointed time. This will mean that I am not worrying about moving money to the right place at certain times of the month, which will do wonders for my stress levels, particularly as this is one of my direct responsibilities.

In terms of when regular payments are paid, make sure that this is in a timely manner and when it suits you. If all your income arrives at the beginning of the month then it makes sense that as much as possible of the outgoings are taken out of the bank just after this. Streamline this to work for you and to suit your business.

Tip:

Spend a little bit of time checking your bank account to make sure that you do actually pay everyone on your payee list. I find that even people who have been paid once are still on there and, as it is unlikely that they will be paid again, they can be deleted from the bank account, making that a tidy place too.

Suppliers – who do you supply to and who do you take supplies from on a regular basis?

Make an inventory of your suppliers, like a Yellow Pages advert with name, phone number, email address, what they supply and when, e.g. paper towels, monthly. This will be an invaluable resource for your business both now and the future, if kept updated. It is very useful for others to know which companies you currently prefer as your supplier of various goods and how they are paid, e.g. invoice or by card.

Review

Put in a review time as this will ensure that you are getting best value from all your suppliers at all times. Let them know you review it all as well, as it may come in handy. Mark this in your calendar, so that it comes round as one of the regular jobs. You know what they say: 'If you look after the pennies the pounds will look after themselves.'

Invoices

There are many ways of doing invoices using online systems. These can be linked into your bank reconciliation systems as well, for example using Xero or QuickBooks. We use Xero but we also have to issue old-fashioned receipts and invoices to some customers, such as local authorities where they have been slow to change to online banking and systems. In addition, we still work with two local authorities who insist on having cheques issued for payments due, which has meant that we still have to send invoices via post in some cases.

This is not my preferred way of working but as they are our customers and *they* cannot work in any other way, *we* have to work with this. Having spoken to a number of business people, I have discovered that we are not alone. Although we all want to be paperless in invoicing and speedy in payment, they too find that the invoicing method depends on who they are working with. I have outlined the method of invoicing used when we are unable to use an online system.

I prefer to do all invoices on Excel spreadsheets and store them electronically, with clear dating etc., so that you can find them easily. The reason I like Excel for invoices is that you can set up the formulas to work out payments due to you and then use the format with the formula by 'saving as' and reusing for different invoices. It also provides a continuity that customers are familiar with. The labelling and dating of these spreadsheets should be easy to sort out, without having to open any up to see which one it is.

We have a labelling system developed years ago which has two letters, some numbers, then two letters at the end. The first two letters refer to who is sending the invoice, so in my case it would be TB. Then there is a six-figure date, which refers to the date the invoice was issued, followed by a two-figure number which is the number of the invoice done that day; the last two letters refer to who the invoice is to.

So, if you wanted to adopt a similar system and your invoice number was TB11041903WM, I would know that the company TB has sent out this invoice on 11

April 2019 and it was the third invoice done that day, the recipient being a customer with the initials WM. For time-saving reasons, we usually do a number of invoices in a batch on the same day, the one in the example being the third one done that day.

Payment checklist on a spreadsheet

When sending out invoices it is important to have a record of when they went out, to whom and for how much, in order to keep ahead with your management accounts. By keeping all your finances in check, you are in a position to chase up any unpaid invoices. We are quite religious about this, first starting to track all our payments some years ago.

A local authority we were involved with owed us a large amount of money. We needed the money to pay wages and had asked for the invoices to be paid several months beforehand. To cut a long story short, we ended up borrowing against the debt and it was harrowing and stressful for me, as I didn't have the money to pay the wages. For an organization as large as a local authority, this is inexcusable, but this was the position we found ourselves in. I was just a short step away from insolvency, due to non-payment of debts. It was a difficult time. Several times a day I would ring to ask if the money would be coming through.

What we learned from this was two things. Firstly, don't have just one big customer, as we did at the time, because if they choose for unknown reasons to withhold your money, you have nowhere to turn apart from expensive bridging finance. Secondly, I found out that large companies and organizations are obliged to pay small companies in a timely manner, due to the Prompt Payment Code 2008. From September 2019, new government rules came into force, designed to make sure large government suppliers pay their bills to their own suppliers on time.

We now keep a spreadsheet, adding to it as soon as invoices go out to ensure that companies we use are compliant with our payment terms. In addition, and due to being put in this position by such a large local authority customer, we have changed our business structure so that we are no longer so reliant on just one income source.

Do you have staggered debt collection procedures?

We have clear lines of communication about debts owed and the next steps. This again is something that has come from experience. You need to be mindful of the law, but can easily send out debt letter one, two and three before court action. We have standard letters that we issue depending on the debt. Our customers are also prevented from using our service, which usually helps to get fees paid on time.

Recording payments for self-auditing purposes

Use a tracker spreadsheet to record when payments are due. This will help with your cash flow expectations and enables you to chase up any late payments quickly. Keep on top of customer accounts by using a spreadsheet or a bespoke or off-the-shelf system. Set aside a regular time to check up on all payments, either yourself or pass on to a colleague. It's really important that you understand where your money is coming from and when.

Tip:

When reconciling your bank accounts against what comes in and goes out, I keep a running commentary month by month of what the unusual payments in or out mean. This is so that I don't forget when it comes to the end of year and makes the accountant's job a little bit easier (and cheaper?). I use a very simple format – just a new page for each month and it's only to explain what is in the bank account that will need an explanation at the end of the year. For example, if there had to be a refund to a customer, what that was for?

Get your end of year books prepared monthly

As you are already working on the above finance tasks, you may as well go the extra mile and get everything ready for the end of year accounts at the same time. In the past I found that getting everything together ready for the accountants each year was an onerous task. Like lost or missing receipts, or mysterious bank items, with no one remembering what they were for. We now take on this task monthly, getting everything ready in a folder to send off. At the end of the year we just have one month as usual to contend with. So many people get hung up on this and it makes sense to do it whilst things are fresh in your mind.

The end of year folder

The end of year folder also contains digital copies of each invoice, linked to your bank accounts. This makes business life simpler and is an easy reconciliation routine to get into. One of the benefits of using this system is no more lost invoices. By keeping up to date, you are also able to keep ahead of your finances. In our case, the original invoices are kept in plastic wallets in a filing cabinet, separated by months, in case anyone wants to see them. What was once a very stressful task is now part of the routine of storing invoices and reconciling bank statements. For the end of year, we also put a copy of the bank statement into the same online folder to send to the accountants.

Management targets

You can work out your break-even points and then set the targets you need to reach each month. The key here is to document why you need this amount of money by looking at expenses plus contingency. If you get a system going that incorporates a regular routine looking at your numbers, it keeps everything fresh in your mind. This then keeps you in control of the finances.

Once a year

Archive last year's numbers and invoices etc. on your computer, accessible, but away from where you are currently working. If there is a lot of data, you could download it onto a hard drive to store securely. This means that you will only be working with the current year and it simplifies your computer systems.

Tip:

Make sure that you have a current ICO (Information Commissioner's Office) certificate, as you may be keeping customer details in your system. That will be stored in Paperwork, of course.

Summary

I have outlined the sort of things that we put into our Finance folder on the computer. What you put in will be different. The main point to remember is that you are looking for simplicity. The title of your folder is Finance, perhaps with two sub-folders: Accounts and Management. Everything that you do in Finance should fit into one of these two folders, enabling quick access.

Folder Two: Paperwork

Now that you have the structure for your Finance folder, the next one is for paperwork. Your aim is to minimize use of actual paper by storing everything online. This folder, although called Paperwork, includes mostly scanned, downloaded and saved documents in your chosen online storage area.

Online paperwork

Every business has paperwork but nowadays the 'paperwork' is online and accessible from everywhere. Make sure that yours is. No one wants to lose a piece of important paper. Labelling is key.

Tip:

Don't waste time opening documents which could be better labelled. You should be able to tell from the document name what is in it.

Document and review

As stated above, you will need to document all the bits of paper you need to run your business and why you need it, how it fits into the smooth running of the business, and when you are likely to need this paperwork. For example, we review all our policies and procedures once a year. If we need to add anything during the year then, obviously, we do that at the time but usually we review everything in January. By doing this we know that this is a job for that month and we know that everything has been reviewed and/or amended at least once a year.

A word about sequencing

You already know which things go in which order, as you are familiar with what you do on a daily or weekly basis. However, this needs to be documented so that others can follow the exact same system in your absence. For example, if on the second Tuesday of each month, you send out a newsletter to your customers, then this needs to be documented – not only that you do it, but also which program you use to do it, fonts, etc., templates.

All of this will save time for anyone taking over the business or for your staff if they are assigned the role of sending out the newsletter. By paying attention to this level of detail, you are going to a) make it easy for someone to follow, b) ensure that they are successful and c) maintain a familiar format that works for your business.

Tip:

We use our email inbox as the anchor in the business and this makes everything really easy. Nothing is taken out of the inbox until it is dealt with and we have a powerful search facility on there so that everything can be found.

Your calendar

Your calendar can become your 'easy to follow' workload assistant, if you set it up correctly. Set up notifications to come into the email inbox, as reminders to do tasks. If we follow the rule of leaving them in the inbox until they are completed, it ensures that all jobs get done in a timely manner. Let technology do the work for you.

Office tasks

Set up an 'office tasks' spreadsheet that has everything to do on it, so you can see all tasks in one place. Use a traffic light system to see at a glance what tasks need to be done on a daily, weekly or monthly basis. Set reminders on your email-linked calendar, so that everything goes directly into the inbox. When you are setting up your office task list, think carefully about the sequence or order of tasks. When you have completed it, you can check that you haven't put all the jobs to be done on one day or put lots of items at the beginning or end of the month leaving little to do in the middle.

It's about spreading the workload. You know when your busy times are. For example, you may not do any admin tasks on a Monday, if Mondays are really busy at your office dealing with emails and calls. It might be that you also allocate certain tasks to individuals. In doing this, you will be sharing the workload and accountability. Talking of accountability, we use an office task sheet, and like all of our spreadsheets, we keep them in the 'cloud', on Dropbox. This means that a manager can access Dropbox to check staff progress on tasks on the office task planner, as they will be colouring in the cells using the traffic light system.

Policies and procedures

Your work policies will need to be in this section as well. Make sure you have included everything needed for your business. Make packs that include the relevant policies to be sent by email, if necessary, to new customers or employees, with an invitation to read all your policies, if appropriate, or store on your website for easy access.

For example, when we recruit a new member of staff, we have a new starter checklist, which we keep in our People section, to send out via email to new staff. It is a pack we have put together with a checklist to make sure that all the relevant information is returned. Policies regarding payment terms, terms and conditions and data protection are particularly useful to send out to new customers. Suppliers can also be treated to a similar pack that points out your payment terms.

Contracts and agreements

Contracts and agreements between yourself and customers or suppliers should also be stored and filed, with copies going to all those who need to be bound by them. People say that they read terms and conditions, but they don't, so if there's anything unusual in your Ts and Cs, flag this up separately to them beforehand, so that they don't feel they have missed something. Outside agreements, e.g. leases, should also be stored electronically, clearly labelled so that they are easy to find.

Tip:

I suggest that, wherever possible, you do all things in writing by email. Even if you have a telephone conversation with someone, follow it up with a brief email, clarifying what was said or agreed etc. This can prove invaluable in the future in case of any confusion about what was said at the time, as they have a chance to disagree with you straightaway, if their version of the conversation was different. If your email search system is good, it's fine to leave the document in there, or you may want to add it to a specific file elsewhere.

Insurance

Insurance certificates for employer liability need to be kept for years, depending on your industry and insurance company. Accreditation certificates need to be displayed and kept once they have expired in case you change company to prove that you have had continuous insurance. Old certificates can be scanned and kept online in a relevant folder. You are legally bound to keep details about your business finance and employees for certain periods of time. In our childcare business we also have to keep children's records for many years. Each industry is different. Find out what you need to keep and decide how to keep it.

Special arrangements

In addition, if you have any special arrangements with certain customers for any reason, this needs to be documented so that others can see and continue with it if need be. This also links to special payment details if they are paying off a debt.

Health and safety

You can outsource health and safety requirements if you prefer, or document how and when to do certain checks, like legionella checks on water tanks, fire testing equipment etc. If you take on this task yourself, you will need to be vigilant about keeping records stating what needs doing when, and the qualifications of those carrying out the work on your behalf. Sometimes, this is an area that is easier to outsource as some tasks require specialist knowledge and training. Where health and safety are concerned, do not get it wrong as you could end up being fined or, in some cases, sent to prison. If in doubt, pay the money and outsource it. You don't need the stress.

Summary

Over the years you will gather data or paperwork for a variety of reasons. It is vital, therefore, that you develop a robust and easy to understand online system. We moved to a largely paperless office when the storage of our documentation, which has to be kept for many years in my industry, was becoming an issue and costing us a lot of money. Now that we have made the switch, I don't know why it wasn't done sooner. I can access my documents from anywhere and don't need to worry about physical storage issues.

Folder Three: People

The last element in this phase is the folder on people. This mostly concerns employees, so may or may not be relevant to your business.

Staff documentation

There is a whole load of documentation that you need to save for your workforce. This includes their contract of employment, personal details etc. In addition, as an employer, you are also responsible for making sure they have a right to work in this country and that their qualifications are up to the local standard. Keep all documentation in individual staff folders and ensure that you have everything in place for each member of your team.

Tip:

When keeping records on your staff, which you are legally obliged to do, remember that they have a right to see what you have on file about them, so be sure that this is fact and not opinion.

Staff discipline

You need to keep details of disciplinary action on staff files for a certain amount of time, depending on your company policies. You are also advised to keep minutes of meetings that led to the decision to take disciplinary action. Keeping a record of staff absence and late arrivals is also recommended. It's no good saying to them that you think they have been late three times last week; you will need the evidence to back up your claim with times etc. It is good practice to keep these records.

References

This information also comes in handy when you are required to give a member of staff a reference for another job, or not. You are not obliged to give a reference to anyone but it is good practice to follow your own policy on references for staff to ensure consistency. You might decide to write a reference for a staff member when they have left your company, even if they have not requested one. This is useful to keep on their file and makes the process of giving an accurate reference swift. For more information about what you can and cannot say in a reference, visit acas.org.uk.

Holidays

All employees are entitled to annual leave. When they request holiday time, it needs to be logged in their file as well, so that all their details are in one place. Granting a request for annual leave will depend on how you operate your holiday allocations (e.g. only one person on holiday at a time). Holiday forms or requests for annual leave should be stored in your People file, so that you can easily access and send a form, when required. You will need a documented tracking system to make sure that they have their correct holiday entitlement – not too much or too little. You can access the government website to work out individual staff holiday entitlement. Storing documents to do with people in the People folder makes them easier to locate, even if it is 'paperwork' that you are storing.

Working hours

Staff working hours may need to be logged so that you can pay them. This is an area you can outsource. If you don't feel confident with this aspect of your business, get a company in to do it. They will look at all the nuances of paying people, for example sick pay, parental leave entitlement and payment. You will have to pay for this service, but it could be something that saves you time and money (and headaches!) in the long run.

Online wage slip

When it comes to paying staff, I suggest an online wage slip. This is something that we have adopted recently within my company. Prior to this we had to have wage slips printed out and delivered to sites where people were working by individual managers. Sometimes this fitted in with their routine, but sometimes staff were either getting their wage slips late or managers were going out just to deliver wage slips.

In addition, we also had one or two issues where wage slips had been sent in the post but people said they hadn't received them, or had lost them. The new online wage slips now ensure that everyone gets their wage slip and wages at exactly the same time and there is no chance of losing them or someone claiming that they haven't received them. This new online system also allows you to track whether people have had their wage slip and when it was delivered etc.

Paying wages

We pay wages on a certain day each month and this is one of the jobs I have kept, along with reconciling the finances and making payments. There is a sheet with all dates throughout the year that staff will be paid and when they will receive their wage slip (due to weekends and bank holidays sometimes the date is slightly variable). The accountants email individuals with their wage slips the day before the wages go into their bank accounts. Wages information is also put onto the work calendar, which then feeds through to the email inbox. Staff wages is one of the areas I still oversee, but of course for many of you this would be another area to outsource.

Summary

If you have employees in your business, I would recommend that they each have an online folder with their information and copies of certificates in it. This is the place to keep their contracts and any other information about them, including references. If setting up, working out and paying wages seems like a big job, outsource some or all of it. The main idea, as usual with any of these folders, is that whatever you do (or whoever does it), how and when to do each step is documented.

Conclusion to Phase Four

No one wants your job. Nobody is contemplating buying your business so that they can slip into your shoes and take on your workload, unless of course your workload and role in the business is minimal. This has been the aim of this phase. Buyers want to take over a smooth running, profitable business where they can add their own ideas and take the success of the current business forward. By systemizing as much as possible in the business in a simple way you will make your business more attractive to buyers.

The Three Folder System puts everything about your business into one of three areas – Finance, Paperwork or People

– making it easy to understand. Planning your business systems and how they work around these three areas is the key to making your business more efficient. The Systems Revision Sheet helps you decide what is relevant for your business to systemize. Fundamental to the Three Folder System working for your business is removing the individuals (including you) and concentrating on the tasks, leaving a systemized business which anyone can follow. This will make it very attractive to prospective buyers.

Chapter takeaways

Finance
- Track all money in through the bank
- If you can, get rid of cash in your business
- Review your suppliers regularly
- Have a checklist to ensure payments are made
- Prepare end of year books each month
- Get into regular routine reconciliation

Paperwork
- Be clear on labelling documents and folders
- Spread the workload
- Use an office tasks spreadsheet
- Make staff accountable for their own tasks
- If in doubt, outsource (health and safety)

People

- Assign each staff member an online folder for all the information you have about them
- Remember they can request to see their file (so keep it factual)
- Consider online wage slips
- Work out when you need to pay wages in advance

Call to action

Put all your systems into one of the Three Folders.

Phase Five

Making a decision

Introduction

Having worked your way through the book and Workbook so far, you may be closer to having an idea about whether you are in a position to retire. In Phase Three you worked out your financial position and how this would impact on your retirement. As part of that you were encouraged to add in your own business numbers. For some of you, retirement means selling your business to release the funds. In this last phase, we look at the two main options for you and your business. To sell or not to sell.

Chapter Eight

To sell

If you have made the decision to sell, follow the six simple steps to selling below to ensure you achieve the best sale for you and your business.

Business sale: the six simple steps to selling

1. Sell your business for what you think it's worth or don't sell at all
2. Sell your business to suit your timing or don't sell at all
3. Make sure you leave your business in a happy state
4. Do alright by your employees, suppliers and customers when selling
5. Make it easy for the buyer to continue trading as you would wish
6. Make sure you have your next plan in place with contingencies

By looking at these six simple steps when selling, you can ensure that you leave your business as you would want to leave it, when you want to leave it. There's a lot to be said for peace of mind in retirement and its effects on your ongoing mental well-being.

1. Sell your business for what you think it's worth or don't sell at all

We have already talked about valuing your business in Phase Three, including discussing vanity valuations. Don't fall into the trap of needing a certain unachievable amount for your business. Look, instead, for another way, rather than selling out at rock bottom.

Let's say that you go into the shop for a loaf of bread which costs £1.25. You give the cashier a £5.00 note and she gives you £2.75 change and your receipt. You glance at your change and put it into your pocket. When you get home your son asks for £3.50 for the bus. You reach into your pocket and you don't have enough for him. You realize you have been short-changed. How do you feel? Annoyed? Upset? Daft?

Annoyed with the cashier for short-changing you – even if it was a genuine mistake on her part? Upset that you now don't have enough cash for your son, so you have to find him a fiver (and know you won't see any change from that either!)? Daft for not checking the change more diligently whilst you were in the shop, where it could have easily been rectified? You get the idea. You don't want to end up feeling short-changed by someone who has bought your business for something less than you think it is worth. You will always feel the pain.

2. Sell your business to suit your timing or don't sell at all

I have a dream. I have a dream that one day someone will come along and make me an offer for my business that I really cannot refuse. The new purchaser fits in with my expectations and values and is a good fit for all my staff and customers. But the catch is they want me to go by the end of the week. As I said, I have a dream. This is a lovely daydream where everything is hunky-dory. The buyer rides in on a white horse, aligning with your values and exceeding your financial expectations. In addition, they take all the legal, accountancy and professional strain away from you, in order to acquire the business. They then leave you with pots of money (too much in fact)… but it is just that, a dream.

Unfortunately, for the vast majority of us, this will not happen. No one will come in to take away the pressure and anxiety of selling your business. No one will work out exactly what is best for your business, your future finances, your family circumstances and your well-being, apart from you. The ball is in your court.

No one out there will even know that your business is for sale until you tell them (apart from those blokes riding through town on white horses!). The positive point in all of this is that the timing of when you sell your business is going to be your call. This may depend on a number of factors:

- Your age
- Your retirement age
- If your business has 'seasons' (some businesses are busier at different times of the year)
- When your financial year ends
- The state of your last set of accounts
- Staffing factors
- Pension pots and whether they are aligned at the moment
- Your income requirements now and in retirement
- Whether you have got your business ready for sale
- Your health and/or that of someone close to you
- Your current projects and business plans
- Whether you are ready mentally

3. Make sure you leave your business in a happy state

Linking back to mental well-being, it is important that you leave your business because you are happy to do so and that the business is in a happy state. By this, I mean that you feel comfortable leaving it and this could be a sale, a management buy-out, or just closing it down. The last thing you want to feel is regret. Regarding your employees, customers and suppliers, my personal yardstick is 'would I be happy to bump into them in the supermarket?' The answer should be yes from your point of view.

Obviously, there are some people that you don't want to catch up with but that could be for any number of reasons. You should have no regrets that the person you bump into will think that you did anything but your best for them, at the time. If you have ensured that you have done your best by people and treated them fairly (whilst looking after yourself), then you will have no regrets. In addition, by planning carefully for your retirement, you should be in a happy state of mind for the next stage of your life.

4. Do alright by your employees, suppliers and customers when selling

This links directly with the above. By 'do alright' I mean don't leave any loose ends, make sure you pay any outstanding invoices, check that replies have been made satisfactorily to emails. Make sure the new person taking over has an overview of your relationships with people and the do's and don'ts of the business. This will make a smooth transition for customers, suppliers and employees and will make you feel that you have done your best to accommodate everyone before you left.

After this point, when you have done all you can, it is all documented and you have followed your own plan for retirement, with explanations for everything and everything covered – relax. You can do no more. You are not responsible for any actions taken by the next person to do your job. You are not responsible for any relationship build-up or breakdown that follows. It is not in your power to fix or mend new relationships and contracts.

You must let the new people involved in your business work it out for themselves, work on their own relationships and, of course, make their own mistakes, as that is how they will learn. You have mitigated against any mistakes and now it is time to watch them fly. However, if they crash and burn, it's not your fault or responsibility. It's a bit of a tough one. But at some point, you just have to let go. After all, this is about you, your needs, your family needs, your retirement and your life beyond this business.

5. Make it easy for the buyer to continue trading as you would wish

Throughout this book you have seen the importance of setting your business up for sale in terms of systems and record keeping, with the Sum Up Report for people to follow if they choose. You can only lead a horse to water; you cannot make it drink. It must also be recognized that you are not just doing this for them and for the future good health (as you see it) of the business; you are also doing it for yourself and your peace of mind.

When the job is done and you feel that you can do no more, you will be able to rest and relax and enjoy the next phase of your life, with or without your business. Don't be surprised if the new owner changes most things – they want control, they want to assert their will and they want to do it better and more profitably than you have (and they think they can!). Most people who buy a business don't think, 'Great! I can sit back and leave this one ticking over'. They want to change things, put in their own ideas, possibly their own staff, suppliers and ways of doing things.

Your way, your work, your systems, your SWOT analysis have probably given them some good ideas so far and they will be grateful to take over a good, happy, going concern, which they know works. But it's more than likely they will still want to make it feel like their own. This is natural and to be expected and there is nothing you can do about it apart from preparing the people in your business, but most of all preparing yourself, for the changes to come. You may become so far removed that you are not even aware of any changes.

6. Make sure you have your next plan in place with contingencies

We've already talked a lot about getting the right plan for you in place. What you will need to think about now are contingencies. I regard contingencies as a part of the planning process. It doesn't hurt to be one step ahead and working out your next move in case of a 'What If' scenario. Let me explain.

Contingency planning

Some time ago it looked like I was going to lose my business without having the opportunity of selling it. My first thoughts were: disaster, how can we manage, what will we do? I knew (and know) that I will never work for anyone so it was going to be up to me to either work out a new retirement plan, a little too early, or work out how to make additional income without having to become an employee. So I did both.

By re-examining our household expenditure and when pensions were expected to start, I managed to make it OK (just about) if we lost everything in one go. We wouldn't have the travel I wanted, we wouldn't have the same income or the same freedom, but I had worked out a way to make better use of an asset we already had, to increase our monthly income to make up some of the shortfall. After my initial panic, I was able to see a way through this potential 'disaster'.

Needless to say, I was over-reacting and we didn't need to change too much of our original plan. However, I was quite pleased that, although it would be different, it wouldn't be such a bad thing to change the plan and we would be able to cope (without taking on paid employment!). I suppose that I was building contingency into the plan.

If you are able to think about the 'What If' scenarios before they happen, this will give you confidence in yourself and your original plan. In addition to building in contingencies for the future, like needing a new car, special occasions like weddings etc., you should also look at what would happen, for example, if your pension didn't hit a certain target.

The last word on contingency is to make sure that none of your decisions, financial or business, leave you in a static position. You need a little bit of leeway for the things that we cannot foresee and/or know are out there (a recession for example).

Mental health in retirement

For many, particularly business owners who have been used to making decisions about themselves, their employees and company every day, sometimes every hour of every day, this first stage of retirement can be particularly tricky. You have been used to being in charge; you have been identified by your role at work; you have enjoyed respect from colleagues and fellow workers. You are in charge.

On the evening of your last day at work, you will no longer be the boss; no longer have to turn up to work come-what-may (illness, car broken down, children sick); no longer be on the end of the phone when things don't go right at work; no longer be questioned for your knowledge; no longer enjoy your status in the community as a company boss; no longer be invited to business functions, and therefore maybe, no longer be you. For most of us our identity is wrapped up in our work.

Think about how you are introduced to people: 'This is Terri, she's the boss'; 'This is Terri, she has had her own company for 20 years. Your identity and work go together, as they do in all walks of life': 'So and so is a teacher'; 'My mum works at the bakery'; 'I want to be a policeman when I grow up'. Our lives are intertwined with our work identities. When this is taken away, many people, even those who have prepared for this for some time, feel an acute sense of loss.

So, you need to be prepared mentally to take on the challenge of retirement. You will need to seek out new purposes, new friends and activities, a new timetable, a new routine, and perhaps learn new skills. Your positive mental attitude towards this part of your life is really important in ensuring your mental health and well-being. Some people may be scornful that retirement would affect them in anything less than a positive way. However, we must be cautious with ourselves, so that we plan for both the positive aspects of retirement (no mortgage, travel opportunities, more time with grandkids etc.) and possibly the less positive side of identity loss, new beginnings and changes, like less money.

Retire well

One of the best ways to prepare for this is to retire well. This sounds obvious but we can lessen the risk of adversely affecting our mental health in retirement by good planning in a few areas.

Conclusion

If you have made a decision, financially or otherwise, to sell your business, you need to look at the benefits that this will bring. I am assuming you are selling for a price you are happy with and that this money will contribute to your long-term future. You are now in a position to start thinking about what you will do with all this new-found time and freedom.

If you check out Google, you can find lots of advice on retirement activities. After sorting out their financial commitments (mortgage etc.), lots of new retirees like to travel, particularly if they missed out on travelling at a younger age – perhaps because they were building the business? Travel is a great way to broaden your horizons, have new adventures and meet new people.

For some of you, it may be that you wish to (or have to) take on a small job. This will keep you in the loop with society, and for some people gives a regular purpose every day. Others may become volunteers and give their services for no financial reward but still enjoy being part of a business, for example, working in a charity shop or similar. For others, they have waited until retirement to have the freedom to follow their hobbies, perhaps started in working life and neglected due to work commitments. If you sell your business, I am suggesting that you need something to do in your new role, remembering the part that your mental health and well-being plays in this.

Chapter takeaways

- Consider the six steps to selling
- Try to do 'right' by everyone connected to your business
- Have contingencies in place
- Think about yourself and retire well

Call to action

Consider how you can implement each of the six steps to selling.

Chapter Nine

...Not to sell

At the beginning of this phase, we talked about the only two options for you and your small business – to sell or not to sell. What would it be like if you didn't sell your business?

It makes sense that in order to realize your expected pension income you need to sell your business. But what if you could achieve that expected pension income without selling your business or working in your business?

By reading through this book and taking on the principles in it, you have seen your business laid bare. You know exactly what it can achieve; you know the opportunities and threats. You have mitigated against them, given reasons for your business weaknesses and elaborated on the business strengths. You have worked on getting it ready for sale, by putting all the systems in place, making sure that everything is documented for staff.

Now that your business is in excellent shape, you may decide to keep it. Instead of you moving out of your business, making sure that no one has to do your job, what about you not doing your job but still reaping the rewards of the business you have spent so long building up?

Bear with me and I will explain. You now know how much money you need for your retirement and no doubt that was based on your current income. What about if your current income stayed the same or was slightly different, but you didn't need to sell your business in order to achieve it? Can you have both income and freedom? You can. If you take *fretirement*, rather than retirement, you can do just that.

What is fretirement?

The new word fretirement *is made up of two words, retirement and freedom.*

Therefore, my definition of fretirement *is:*

Having the freedom to 'retire' from your business without giving it up.

We get so involved in our own businesses and our own little worlds that we forget how far we've come. We don't appreciate what our business gives us in many ways. Let me elaborate. Currently your business gives you a regular income, possibly other incomes, e.g. pension contributions and family wages, a car? However, on the negative side, it can also give you stress, which may have led you to feel that you need to get out (often at whatever cost) unless approached differently.

Think about it this way. If you were to sell, you wouldn't have a business. If you put yourself in that position for a moment of not having a business, what sort of feelings does that conjure up? I know we all say things like: 'It would be great not having to get up in the morning, a relief not having to deal with the staff, or money, or complaints, or orders', or whatever it is you deal with... Then don't.

Train your staff, put highly organized and foolproof systems in place, buy in more help, outsource the jobs you don't like, take yourself out as if you have sold the business, but still reap the benefits of all your hard work. Fretirement is exactly that. Giving you the freedom to 'retire' in whatever way you choose. Allowing you to work as little or as much as you want in a business that you know really well. Don't get me wrong: I am asking you to make a huge shift in your thinking, not least of all, not being in charge, and this is very hard. But it is achievable. It also doesn't happen overnight. You have to work at it. But you will have to work hard whether you sell or stay, so no option is easier.

If you can't face selling your business or don't really want to, you can work differently (or not at all). For example, you could reduce your hours within your business by working part time. You could employ someone or several people, either in the business or by outsourcing specific job roles, thereby releasing some time for yourself. You can look at what hours you would like to do, implement further systems or put in bespoke ones to release you from the hours you currently do. This will not happen overnight but is something that you can work towards.

In one of my businesses we used to have an office team of between three and five people at any one time. As part of a longer-term plan we worked hard to develop, alongside outside agencies, an online bespoke system. Our customers could access this remotely, therefore removing the need to speak to admin staff. As part of this plan, as staff have left the company we have not replaced them, relying more heavily on our bespoke system. This has made our system and business more efficient in terms of professionalism as well as working towards being paperless. As a manager it has meant fewer hours required to supervise staff. Having this system in place has effectively reduced my hours and as this was part of the plan going forward, those hours have not been replaced by other roles I could have taken on in the business. Instead, they have been used for my next stage – writing my books.

As your business becomes more streamlined, there are more and more opportunities to develop yourself in other ways without the need to let go of your business, or the income it provides. It just takes careful planning. By re-organizing your business finances you can decide exactly how much income you take and how much goes to others running parts of your business in-house or outsourcing.

This is perfectly possible. Who knew? Who knew that you could have your cake and eat it?

Disadvantages and advantages

Sell and retire if you can make your retirement figures work and you truly want to get out. Fretire if you are not really ready to retire but would like a retirement lifestyle and join those in fretirement who have built their business to work for them for longer.

This fretirement approach should also be explored as you work out what to do in your next stage of life. There are advantages and disadvantages to fretirement and we will explore both. Let's start with the disadvantages of fretirement.

Disadvantages of fretirement

- You don't get a lump sum from selling your business
- You may feel that you can't let go
- You may still have a sense of responsibility
- You will need to work out clear details before taking this step, which is time-consuming
- You will have to trust and accept other people's judgement
- You will need to train others extensively to achieve a good fretirement, again which is time-consuming
- You might not like the lack of control

Disadvantages unpicked

You don't get a lump sum from selling your business

Now, this may seem like stating the obvious, but it will impact on your finances right at the beginning.

Most people use their lump sum from any pension pot (remember you can take 25% tax free) and use it to pay off any large financial commitments, e.g. loans, mortgages. Lots of people like to free up their mortgage commitment so that they don't feel burdened to a lender. Also, they won't necessarily have the means to pay this off ever again – unless they have a lottery win.

If paying off your mortgage is part of your financial plan and you don't sell your business or have a pension pot to look forward to, overpaying on your mortgage is a good idea and should be part of your financial plan. If you are planning on fretiring, you may be able to continue to pay off your mortgage at its usual rate and it will be paid off in a number of years, agreed at the start, without overpaying. When you are deciding what to do, the amount of your mortgage and monthly amounts need to be catered for.

You may feel that you can't let go

You have been at the head of your business for some time and the thought of not being in charge is weighing heavily on your mind. If you look at the scenario that you have sold the business, then you wouldn't have anything to do with it at this point: you would not be in charge, no one would ask your opinion. This calls for a mind shift. You have to let go for the most part or you may as well sell your business. That is always an option later, if you don't feel you are benefitting from being fretired, due to your own control needs.

You may still have a sense of responsibility

I think that this is a big one. You may find that your team, the one you put in place to take control of the business, is not working out as you had hoped. Is this true or is it that you cannot let go of your responsibilities? From the team's point of view, this is very difficult, as they want to be in charge and have been tasked with looking after the business. If you keep stepping back in, you will undermine confidence in their own ability and probably end up working back in the business or at least making decisions.

This is not retirement, semi-retirement or fretirement. This is work. If you want to work then all well and good, but surely the reason you are reading this book is because you don't want to work any more, in one form or another? It is one of the hardest things to do in my experience: to give control of your 'business baby' to others. They make mistakes, they don't do things in the right way, they are too slow etc., etc. But they are learning how to do things the right way and as part of your training plan you need to account for this.

You will need to work out clear details before taking this step, which is time-consuming

This is not a quick fix. If you are to do this fretirement thing right, it needs careful planning so that you have thought of everything in advance of making any moves. If you are expecting to walk away from reading this book and implement your fretirement next week then I may have news for you. The best way to achieve a good fretirement for you, your employees or those who take over and your business is to spread it out over some time. It may take six months, 12 months or 18 months for you to get yourself and your business ready to run without you. Which is essentially what fretirement is. It might take that long to get everyone used to the idea that you will not be around; it may take that long for you to decide to do it and set up the next stage of your life.

You will have to trust and accept other people's judgement

OK, so we are really pushing your buttons now. In order for you to do what you want to do, if you choose to keep your business, you have to accept that other people are not you. They will possibly cost the business more as well. I'm not talking about wage increases; I'm talking about incidentals, like when you look carefully at spending patterns to cut back.

Let's take an example. You have always shopped around for the best deal on a certain item required by the business, therefore saving the company a little bit of money. You may find a colleague will just go for the first deal that comes up on a search engine regardless of cost, delivery or even quality. This is because it is easier for them to make one phone call or online order, rather than shopping around. I know from experience that this one hurts, so my advice to you is to expect it. Expect that they won't see the value in shopping around, recycling, making do a bit longer, and budget for this in your financial plan on the business side.

It took me a while to get to this one, as it used to make me really cross that others could not see how money was being wasted. My solution was to allow an undisclosed budget in my head, that I saw as part of the financial package of having someone else look after your purchases. This made the process easier once I had decided to see it as a business expense. The person left in charge would overspend, buy unnecessarily or not look after stock. For my own peace of mind, I had to do this to help *me* move on and out.

You will need to train others extensively to achieve a good fretirement, again which is time-consuming

As we have already said, this is not a quick fix. Training people takes time. Sorting out your values and vision for the business's next stage takes time, but if this is your chosen path the rewards are immense. You get to have your cake and eat it.

You might not like the lack of control

Just to re-iterate. You might not like it. That's OK but you will need to work it out in your mind beforehand if you are thinking about fretirement. Don't put all the work and planning into setting this up just to run back at the first glitch. Be confident in your team and have confidence in your plans and training.

Confidence in the team

When I first decided to start on this journey, I was running a childcare company and I knew that Ofsted were due to do a periodic check on our day nursery. I had spent a few months at the beginning of the fretirement journey working with staff, training them and working on the vision and values of the business moving forward.

I went on holiday part way into my training schedule and of course, you guessed it, Ofsted turned up to inspect the provision. They rang at lunchtime to say they would be with us early the next morning, so not much notice. My immediate thoughts on finding this out were to jump on a flight to the UK to take charge of the situation. I decided not to do this as I thought that it would undermine all the work I had been doing in my staff training, placing my confidence in the team to run the business in my absence. It was a very difficult decision and quite a risky one as well, as I was unsure if they were ready.

We spent an afternoon in two separate countries making sure that everything was in order for the inspection. I chose not to go. The staff dealt with this very stressful situation themselves and we got the highest accolade from Ofsted, which is Outstanding. I think that if I had travelled back, my team would have immediately turned to me to take over and would not have had the experience of doing this themselves. It also showed that I had confidence in them, which is what I had been training towards over the last few months. By showing that I had faith in their ability, even in such a risky situation, or despite the risky situation, the staff came through. It was a great test for me as well, but I sort of knew that if I went back to take over, they would never have or feel they had complete responsibility for the business in my absence.

Advantages of fretirement

- No need to sell your business
- Continued regular monthly income
- No agency fees and tax to pay as costs
- Still having a business to sell whenever you like in the future
- You are in control of how much or little you do in the 'new' business
- You can choose to be in control or not
- You can do all the things you wanted to do in retirement, i.e. travelling, in fretirement
- No lack of status
- Toe dipping – this might be a step further towards retirement without going all the way

Advantages unpicked

No need to sell your business

As a small business owner, you have probably spent a lot of time building your business up to achieve a good reputation, decent profits and a regular income for yourself and maybe other family members. When retiring, this is a lot to give up. You must be sure that your predictions for the sale of the business are right, as this affects your future. It is really important that you engage an independent financial advisor when you have done all your calculations etc., as they will be able to tell you if you are right in your predictions and also what you have missed out or forgotten about in your scheme. If, however, you don't sell your business, you will still have it. Planning not to sell your business may be the right thing for you.

You will need to put in rigid systems, checks and balances to minimize the risks involved in not running your business yourself. But once these things are done (and don't be fooled into thinking that this is a quick job), you will be able to fretire happily into the sunset! Phase Four goes into more detail about how to set up the checks and balances to systemize your business. It is also, to a lesser degree, part of your plan to sell your business, so the work is not wasted whichever way you decide to go.

The pull of having a continued regular income for most people is quite significant, particularly if this can be achieved by not working as you were in your business before. Once set up, you can choose your working hours (or none); you can choose your freedoms. True fretirement. Psychologically, this may be a better stepping-stone than selling your business outright and financially it may give the same or a better return than selling your business. Let's look at a made-up scenario to illustrate the point.

In Phase Three we talked about the financial implications of selling your business in detail. In our example, the amount we decided we wanted to achieve to make the figures work for us was a clear £500,000 for the business; that's after tax and fees, so that half a million would be in your pocket. We need to look at how long it would take to make that money if you didn't sell. A simple way of looking at this would be if you and your family wage, plus your work pension, business dividends etc., added up to £100,000 a year, then it would take five years to recoup the money you would have earned from selling your business, *but* as you didn't sell your business, you still have it to sell. Win-win.

But, I hear you say: 'I don't want to run my business any more; that's why I'm thinking about selling!' OK, I get it, so let's look at you taking less than £100,000 out of the business, effectively decreasing your income to say £50,000. (How much were you thinking of living on in retirement from your business sale income?) The additional money would then be used to pay for others to take on the roles that you have vacated. I know that £50,000 is not much, but this could be used to put in additional admin staff and to promote current employees to cover your role or even buy in another person to do your work. It becomes a bit of a minefield and only you will know your numbers and what you can afford to live on comfortably.

Continued regular monthly income

Imagine this. Your bank account is credited with an amount of money on the same day every month, all year. Just think about that for a minute. If you know someone lucky enough to have worked most of their life in a local authority or as a civil servant, this is what happens for them. They reach a certain age and the index-linked pension amount is deposited into their account each and every month, with no work. Perhaps this is the ideal situation. But unfortunately, as a self-employed small business owner, this is probably quite far removed from your situation. So, you have to look at ways to replicate this if a regular monthly income is what you want. As a person in fretirement you can achieve this. You can set the bar, probably set up the payments as well.

No agency fees and tax to pay as costs

This saves you about 30% of the price you would get for your business. As a business person, this kind of figure has to hit a few buttons for you. Although we know that it is good to pay HMRC, as we know it means we are doing well, if there is a way to save money and put it in our own pockets rather than the taxman's then this has to be a positive move.

Still having a business to sell whenever you like in the future

Of course, by going down the fretirement route, you do not sell your business; therefore, you still have a business to sell. Is it true that you can have your cake and eat it? Can you really take an income from your business for as many years as you choose (or forever) and then if you want to, sell the business later to make a lump sum and run? Yes, of course, and why not? You may have a plan which incorporates both fretirement and retirement later. You may try fretirement and want the total freedom and independence that retirement brings so go for full retirement later. Your fretirement options may have something to do with the timing of a business sale or projects you are working on or leases ending. There are many reasons why you would or could work with both options.

You are in control of how much or little you do in the 'new' business

By new business, I mean the business you are creating beyond today that will facilitate your fretirement and how much you are a part of it is entirely up to you. As you are the one setting up the new business with its new rules, you have the opportunity to move tasks to others that are time-consuming or you don't particularly want to do, or you could just give all tasks up if you like. Putting other people in place is difficult as you may feel that they won't do things the way you want them doing and everyone thinks they can run a business – until they start to run a business...

You may have to put in tight controls and checks to ensure that they understand the reasons behind your former business decisions and the rationale for doing things the way you do them. This will be aligned to your priorities and business vision, so you need buy-in from others in order to achieve what you want to achieve. This will be part of your training plan.

You can choose to be in control or not

Which leads nicely on to whether or not you want to be in control of your business or whether you are happy to relinquish control to others or someone else – or some control or some areas of control. Because you are ultimately in control, you get to choose who has what level of control. It's still your business.

You can do all the things you wanted to do in retirement, i.e. travelling, in fretirement

Fretirement is the easiest way to do what you want to do in the next stage of your life and still get paid a regular income for it. You can plan trips away, stay away from work and yet still get paid an income, if you set up your business properly before your fretirement.

No lack of status

For some, this is quite a big one. With work (or your own small business) goes a certain unwritten status and a label for you to hang your life on. With fretirement you can make the best use of your time in a way that you want to, yet you are still a business owner, only in a different way. You can keep your contacts, keep your status as a business leader and even win admiration that you are doing what you want to do with your time without taking a deep cut in income.

Toe dipping

With fretirement you are able to have a go at being retired without the finality of giving up your business. If you don't like it (all this free time, trips abroad and lots more time for hobbies), you can go straight back to your business and carry on. Nothing lost. Hopefully you will not want to do this, but as far as fretiring goes, you could take it in stages and dip your toes in one at a time so to speak. Nothing ventured, nothing gained, as the saying goes.

Commitment, comfort and confidence

Fretirement is about commitment, comfort and confidence.

- Are you committed to setting up and organizing your business systems beforehand to handle this change?
- How comfortable do you feel with handing over tasks and jobs within your organization, which is linked to training of others (another commitment)?
- Do you have confidence in others taking the business forward so that you have the freedom to follow your next stage?

For those of you who need a concrete example or two of how fretirement could look in practice, I have some suggested scenarios below. They cover different levels of fretirement: low, medium and high level, high level being the least hands-on in your business.

Low-level fretirement

You have all the systems in place to run your business, but you are still going into the 'office' several times a week to make sure that everything is OK. You have employed additional staff to run the systems and one of your roles is to manage the people running the systems. You are still the person who is asked for advice and you like to keep in touch with a few key customers. However, you are increasingly away from the workplace doing the things that you want to do.

Medium-level fretirement

You have all the systems in place to run your business and are able to access them remotely, which you do on a regular (weekly or monthly) basis to make sure that everything is going OK. You have people in place to run the business on a day-to-day basis for most things, but you have kept one or two tasks that you enjoy doing or prefer to keep control of yourself. You have commitments around these tasks and sometimes you go into the workplace to perform them, although this is not necessary as you can access any work information online. You have put in a new layer of management that can deal with day-to-day enquiries and you are only asked advice occasionally. You spend more time away from the 'office'; however, you still feel the responsibility.

High level-fretirement

All systems for your business are in place and it is a manager's job to oversee and ensure that everything is going smoothly. All tasks are now outsourced or completed by managers. There are accountability checks within the organization between and amongst managers. You are informed at a regular meeting (annual or bi-annual) of how the company is doing, plus any changes and initiatives. Your role is more of a non-executive director who has an in-depth knowledge of the business. You hardly go to the 'office' as you have staff in place to deal with your business.

The above examples are a guide only and you may see which level, or part of a level, you want to be. There is crossover between the levels and it is up to you to decide where best you fit for your own situation. Is the lack of control of the high level not what you had in mind, or is it something to aspire to? For all of the levels, the business systems are in place to give you the option to perform yourself, in-house or outsource. The choice is yours. Setting out exactly how much you 'earn' within your business is also your choice.

If you don't want to relinquish complete control of your business (perhaps the reason you are not selling?), as in high level, you may find your own level of commitment to the day-to-day running of your business. You need to feel comfortable that your chosen level enables you to get on with the things outside your business that you want to do. And lastly, you need to have the confidence that your business will run as you wish, with or without your input.

Conclusion

Now that the option of not selling your business has been put forward, you are in a position to make some big decisions. Will you sell your business and retire? Is your business ready for this? Are you? Or will you keep your business, fretire and work out what you want your role in the business to be? You have all the advantages and disadvantages before you to help you explore your options, but there's no rush. You have plenty of time to make your mind up. Perhaps this new option needs time to sink in until you get used to it.

Chapter takeaways

Fretirement is about commitment, comfort and confidence.

The definition of fretirement is:

Having the freedom to 'retire' from your business without giving it up.

Disadvantages of fretirement could be:

- No lump sum but no money worries
- Can you let go of your responsibilities?
- You will need to design a clear plan to train others
- Trusting other people's judgement and accepting lack of control

Advantages of fretirement could be:

- Keep your business and a regular income
- No costs or lack of status
- Try 'retiring' before you sell
- Re-organize your workload
- Time and money to do what you want

Call to action

It's now time to think about your next move. Is fretirement an option for you?

Or are you going to sell your business and retire?

Conclusion

It's time for some serious thinking.

I am assuming that the reason you picked up this book was out of curiosity. You were perhaps curious to see whether you had to sell your business in order to retire from it. The answer, of course, is: it depends.

At the beginning of the book the seed was planted suggesting that giving up your business was a possibility. You were encouraged, however, to think carefully about this huge decision, not only in terms of the practicalities but also in terms of your own personal feelings and reasons for wanting to give it up.

By giving you a chance to consider yourself before considering others and your business, you were hopefully able to explore the Five Key Questions in your Workbook. In doing this, you were approaching a possible sale of your business in a completely different way.

The usual route for selling a business is:

1. Decide to sell
2. Get an agent involved to value the business
3. Put the business on the market
4. Sell

However, *The Beginning of the End* takes you through the tiny space of thinking about selling your business *prior* to calling the agent.

As an entrepreneur, I know we view our businesses as family extensions that we have nurtured and carefully tended, often without just reward for many years. The emotional side of selling your business and how that makes you feel is often overlooked and should not be underestimated.

By not allowing yourself to consider the key aspects of selling your business beforehand, you may find yourself in a state of guilt or stress that you are, or are not, doing the right thing. There are many variables to consider and by doing this prior to calling the agent, you give yourself time to think about possible scenarios to make the right decision for your business, staff and for yourself and your family. By looking at the business objectively and considering the Five Key Questions you are able to work out where your sticking points are and where you may have difficulties.

From the thinking stage, you moved on to preparing to sell, again starting with some tricky questions to consider. In order to help you get your business ready for market you prepared a SWOT analysis on your business. Following on from this, you were encouraged to prepare a Sum Up Report for a prospective buyer.

Next, you looked at the business numbers to add to the Sum Up Report, finalizing it ready to help sell your business. The purpose of following this route was to showcase your business a) for any prospective buyer but also b) for yourself.

When looking at your personal pension you saw that income from various small pensions adds up. You were encouraged to work out, using your personal figures, whether selling your business would achieve the income needed to retire comfortably. For some, working this out is a lovely surprise. For others, a huge disappointment that all their hard work over the years seems to amount to less than they were expecting and certainly not enough to give the generous retirement expected.

We then covered systemizing your business, looking at your business from the outside rather than the inside. The strong message that no one wants to buy your job came up here, encouraging you to look at exactly how your business is run, systemizing everything to make it flow easily – either for a new buyer or for yourself and your business going forward.

Having travelled the journey through the book, you are left to consider your next option. Weighing up all that has been said and the tasks you have done whilst reading through the book, your options are now clearer. To sell or not to sell, and if you don't sell, what will your working life look like moving forward? I know that by following this book and working through the Workbook, you are in a good place to decide.

It's now time to plan your next move.

Good luck.